Junia and Dennis could hardly believe their luck that they had come across an artist like me who had already so thoroughly addressed the complexities and challenges that arise when a contemporary figure such as an artist or curator (like me or like them) grapples with their present and a past defined by regimes and wants and needs to make a thing that people look at, read, and watch. Our programming matched rather intimately, and so this is how I became an agent, err, artist for Fluentum, the non-profit private art foundation started by software entrepreneur Markus Hannebauer. Hannebauer has a profitable business from a product called think-cell, a tool you can use in combination with PowerPoint to add charts to your slide presentations. With his profits, Hannebauer decided to begin a foundation to time-based art, a rare endeavor in art collecting, to be housed in this dark tomb where projections are highly visible. More people want paintings and sculptures. This is just how it is.

It's even more interesting than that, though. There are parallel circumstances contributing to the development of materialschrank and this sequel materialoutpost that are eerily familiar. This may not seem interesting, but it may help you to see how these productions became what they are [far too long]. The show at Sweetwater, '|', and Time Without End, were to open in the springtime in their respective years; however, due to the success of the novel coronoavirus, each exhibition was postponed to the following fall, adding months more time to think and research and do the grappling referred to earlier. So because everything is connected to everything else, ~~(dare tell me it isn't)~~ the artist has to figure out how far to go with it, the thing.

Meanwhile, between materialschrank and materialoutpost, there are 600,000 dead, former inhabitants of the United States, and a new president. And I still have never been to Berlin.

These are the players and something about their circumstances. I should warn you that sequels are rarely ever as good as the first movie, and I am not the same person I was a year ago.
[Fin]

materialoutpost ||| (the next part)
Note to self: each part builds from the previous (each part builds from the previous?), note the through-line and main parts.
(Trailer) From the people who brought you materialoutpost, here is materialoutpost |||. So you already know the story, but did you also know this other important thing about the characters you've come to love, a story about how art [some of it] gets made today?

Would you believe me--your protagonist--if I told you I was a double agent (whispered)? It's not uncommon. [Zachary Cahill and Philip von Zweck spoke about this in 2014.] A hybridization has occurred that erodes the romantic idea of the artist. For example, the art 'product' is a result of the artist's choices as well as that of the curators. I, the autonomous, have an allegiance to the thing I do, or what my

D'Ette Nogle, *materialoutpost*, 2021.
Excerpts of unpublished film script. Included in the exhibition *Time Without End*, Fluentum, Berlin, 2021.

subjectivity brings, as well as to the objectives of the institution (and the patron(s)), or it may be the case that the institution is finding a way to get me to serve their interests, hmmm. Zweck notes this is becoming a required tactic, especially for an artist participating from the fringes [like me?]. As a word, tactic is unappealing and really eats at the mystery that is the artist for some people.

A quotation from Peter Sloterdijk, via Cahill and Zweck:

One has heard of double and triple agents who themselves in the end no longer know for whom they were really working and what they were seeking for themselves in this double and triple role playing…On which side do our loyalties lie? Are we agents of the state and of institutions? Or agents of enlightenment? Or agents of monopoly capital? Or agents of our own vital interests that secretly cooperate in constant changing double binds with the state institutions, enlightenment, counter-enlightenment, monopoly capital, socialism, etc., and, in so doing, we forget more and more what we our 'selves' sought in the whole business?

[This is also a highly specialized (inside)job] – type it just like that!

[Sydney Bristow scenes here]

Cahill and Zweck describe types of double-agency like the artist-critic and artist-curator. Another form of double-agency is when you combine your day job and your art. My favorite example of this one would be Jef Geys, but although he could be an example, there's something special about Geys that makes me very reluctant to refer to him as a double agent. Geys examples: Geys was a teacher in Balen Belgium where he taught "positive aesthetics" and incorporated his work and the work of other artists into his classroom. Arguably his work was the work conducted in his classroom. His classroom seems to have been very organic. Students used the blackboard to respond to terms grabbed from public debate. He did a project called *Initiation to Marxism in 1982* that, per Dirk Snauvaert writing about Geys, "listed conflicting theories of Marxism that he had studied comparatively, noting the different concepts that divided the ideological schools of thought which dominated the splintered left intellectual spectrum." [Image saved of classroom in Balen https://www.conceptualfinearts.com/cfa/2021/01/06/jef-geys/] https://jefgeysweblog.wordpress.com/2015/08/26/jef-geys-at-s-m-a-k/He was an integrated person, a singular agent of life as art. He was also deft at distancing himself, as artist, from the structures of art such as the personnel and exhibition logistics. Geys is the opposite of double agent! He called the shots. Speaking of romantic ideas, Cahill and Zweck get a little swept up in the idea of double-agency, even saying that as a mode it strives to "divert the flow of human capital by haunting institutions with *artistic spirit.*" Do you think they were high when they wrote that part? I hope so.

[ART WILL MAKE YOU FREE]

Artists serve themselves for compensation that is symbolic. The freedom we get from self-serving autonomy becomes a basis for self-exploitation, as in *yes, I will work for free because it helps me.* Buzzkill! I'm grabbing this idea from Andrea Fraser [and to be sure, my own life], who, in 1994, delivered remarks on 'project work' or artists working doing projects for institutions in her presentation titled "How to Provide an Artistic Service: An Introduction." I like the straightforwardness of this title. Fraser notes "dependence is the condition of our autonomy" and she says, "if we are always already serving, artistic freedom can only consist in determining for ourselves—to the extent that we can—whom and how we serve. This is, I think, the only course to a less contradictory principle of autonomy."

To whom *am* I accountable? Who is my audience? This gets jumbled up for me, especially because part of my identity is that of public-school teacher, and my time is devoted to that shelter-providing occupation and my artist role [note the connection to Geys here]. *To whom am I accountable*? Right now I will say, the deadline! This has been only a partial account of how art gets made.

End

Cut Scene: 10 years later [from 1994…], Fraser participated in a discussion, "The Artist as Currency," with Rhea Anatas, Gregg Bordowitz, Jutta Koether, and Glenn Ligon. Fraser notes "our participation is an investment in the field…To participate in a field at all is to take the forms of satisfaction it offers—benefit, reward, pleasure, affirmation—as one's object. So what are the forms of satisfaction offered by this field? How are they constructed?..Psychically, the object is fundamentally indifferent; socially, however, objects are produced and institutionalized within fields as specific values, rewards, aspirations and trajectories of satisfaction and achievement."
[*As Lacan put it somewhere, while desire may be a constant force, it's supply that produces demand. – Fraser*]
She continues, "That's a process that takes place in the time of our individual and collective histories. Subjectivity is neither who we were born to be and are forever, nor who we are at any given moment. Subjectivity is produced in time and exists in how we temporalize ourselves in the world, and that also means professionally. I don't believe that we're producing in a kind of social-institutional machine that we've been sucked into—or born into. We have entered into this field and are reproducing it in our everyday lives and actions, in our desires, and in our feelings about what we do. That is where agency comes in."

And here the conversation takes a turn, fitting perfectly with where we're going.
Glenn Ligon chimes in to say, "But I think our —not our, *my* idea of a future is still the past."

[Fraser: "I'm with you on that."]

D'Ette Nogle

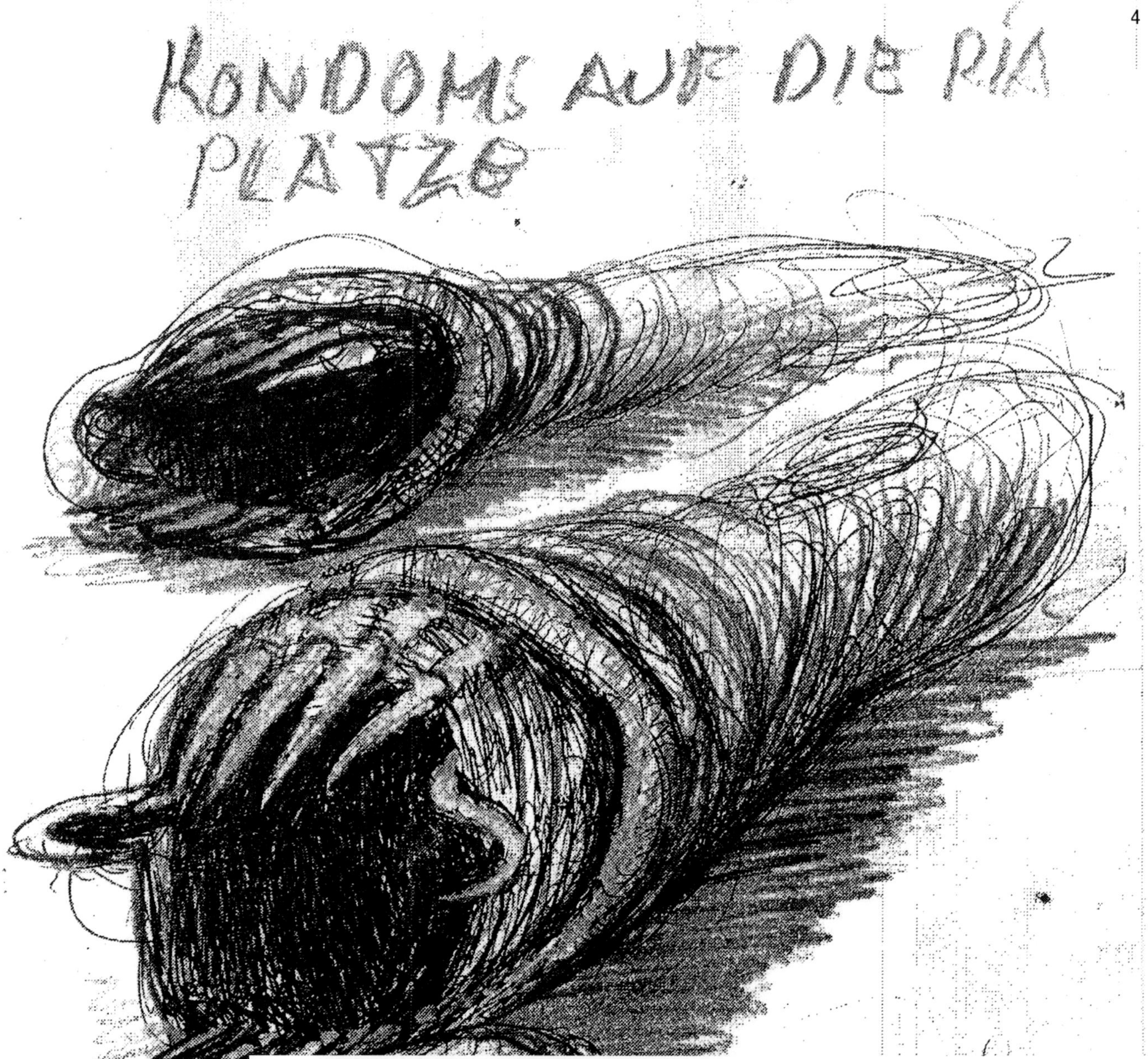

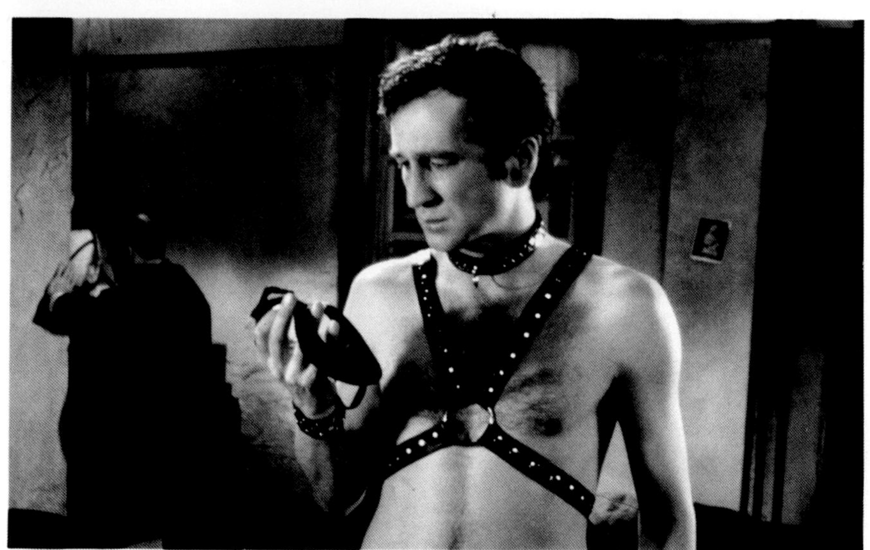

Lloyd Kaufman
&
Michael Herz
present
a Troma Team release
KILLER CONDOM

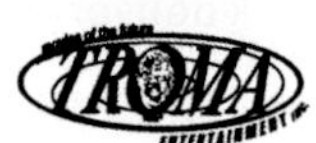

TROMA
ENTERTAINMENT INC.

Elisa R. Linn
No Glove No Love

Martin Walz's *Killer Condom* (*Kondom des Grauens*; 1996) so confidently caters to lowbrow tastes that the film should be awarded the "valuable" rating as an outcast of its time. At first glance a tasteless horror-fantasy metaphor from a pulp novel, the film takes aim at the generic conventions of New American Cinema and mainstream body horror with a dose of "homo promo"[1] in the most curious way—not even forgetting Hitchcock's iconic shower scene from *Psycho* (1960). This urban Western, an adaptation of the eponymous graphic novel (1987) by gay German comics artist Ralf König, features an almost exclusively A-list German-speaking cast cavorting in New York City—which appears here as "a stinking cesspool, a playground for perverts"[2] where penises are castrated.

Udo Samel plays one of them, "beefy" full-blooded Sicilian Luigi Mackeroni, a macho caricature of a film noir detective and a Manhattanite through and through—with a cigarette glued to his lips, tinted glasses, and a proud thirty-two centimeters of manhood—except for one thing: he is unabashedly gay, making him something of a nuisance to the stereotypical image of a toxic hetero cop precinct. As a refresher: just two years after the film's premiere, George Michael released his exuberant single "Outside" (1998), featuring the singer in a police uniform alongside half-nude cops, not on the beat but in an upscale restroom. This was Michael's first time acknowledging his homosexuality "outside" the closet (or rather "toilet") after he was arrested by an undercover officer in 1998 for "lewd acts" in a public restroom in Beverly Hills.

Luigi Mackeroni, who prefers to be called "bull" (slang in German for "cop"), tracks down a fleshy mirage of a complex organism, complete with fine microscopic nerves, a peritrophic membrane, and razor-sharp teeth, despite resistance from his fellow male police officers; he even loses a "nut" in the process. Mackeroni was presumably "semi-emasculated" by his object of desire, the young callboy Billy, who is no longer the virile porn star from the original comic but instead resembles the introverted and wistful street hustler "Mike" in Gus Van Sant's *My Own Private Idaho* (1991)—a melancholic character study that revolutionized the portrayal of male sex workers and ushered in New Queer Cinema.[3] Billy also starkly contrasts with Richard Gere's Julian in *American Gigolo* (1980), a woman-pleasing male sex worker who frowns upon "kinky stuff" and has risen from the world of the abject (i.e., gay, dirty, bad, deviant) to the world of "vanilla sex" (heterosexual, clean, good, as heteronormative as possible).[4] In *Killer Condom*, Billy is not only suspected of a crime because of his immoral career choice: he is much more likely to be under general suspicion precisely *because* he is homosexual and an MSM sex worker.

A fatal misconception, as it turns out, seeing that the Killer Condom actually kills. Purporting to be a functional condom, which resembles today's "Snapchat logo,"[5] it prefers to castrate penis-equipped sex workers in Room 308 of the seedy Quickies love hotel, concealed within unpackaged bulk deliveries of low-price rubbers. Soon, clones

Martin Walz' *Kondom des Grauens* (1996) bedient den niederen Geschmack so selbstsicher, dass der Streifen als verkanntes Schmuddelkind seiner Zeit heute mit dem Prädikat „wertvoll" ausgezeichnet werden sollte. Was wie eine abgeschmackte Horror-Fantasy-Metapher eines Groschenromans anmutet, nimmt mit einer Portion „Homo-Promo"[1] im Mainstream-Kino Filmgenrekonventionen des New American Cinema und Body-Horrors auf kurioseste Weise aufs Korn – wobei auch Hitchcocks ikonische Duschszene aus *Psycho* (1960) nicht fehlen darf. In diesem Großstadtwestern, eine Adaption der gleichnamigen Graphic Novel (1987) des Schwulencomic-Zeichners Ralf König, tummelt sich eine fast durch und durch hochkarätige, deutschsprachige Besetzung in New York – hier „eine einzige stinkende Kloake, in der sich die Perversen tummeln"[2] und Penisse kastriert werden.

Udo Samel spielt einen von ihnen, den „bulligen" Vollblut-Sizilianer Luigi Mackeroni als machistische Karikatur eines Film-Noir-Inspektors, wie er in Manhattan leibt und lebt – mit Dauerkippe, getönter Brille und stolzen 32 Zentimetern Manneskraft, und der besonders eines ist: unverfroren schwul und damit aneckt im generischen Abbild eines heterotoxischen Bullenreviers. Man besinne sich, dass nur zwei Jahre nach dem Release des Films George Michaels triumphale Single *Outside* (1998) herauskam, die den Sänger in Cop-Uniform neben halb strippenden Gesetzeshüterkolleg*innen nicht etwa auf dem Revier, sondern auf einer veredelten Bedürfnisanstalt zeigt. Michael bekannte sich damit erstmals „outside" the closet (beziehungsweise „toilet") zu seiner Homosexualität, nachdem er 1998 wegen „unzüchtiger Handlungen" auf einer öffentlichen Toilette in Beverly Hills von einem Undercover-Polizisten verhaftet wurde.

Luigi Mackeroni, der am liebsten „Bulle" genannt wird, kommt der fleischgewordenen Fata Morgana eines komplexen Organismus mit feinmikroskopischen Nerven, peristropischer Membran und rasierklingenscharfen Beutezähnen trotz aller Widerstände seiner männlichen Polizeikollegen auf die Spur – und verliert dabei sogar selbst ein „Ei". Halb „entmannt" wurde Mackeroni mutmaßlich von seinem Objekt der Begierde, dem Callboy-Jüngling Billy, der, anders als im Originalcomic, hier keinen potenzstrotzenden Pornostar darstellt, sondern eher dem introvertierten und wehmütigen Street-Hustler Mike in Gus Van Sants *My Own Private Idaho* (1991) nahekommt – eine melancholische Charakterstudie, welche die Darstellung von männlichen Sexarbeitern revolutionierte und das New Queer Cinema einleitete.[3] Anders als Richard Gere alias Julian in *American Gigolo* (1980), der einen frauenbeglückenden männlichen Sexarbeiter spielt, der „kinky stuff" verpönt und aus der Welt des Abjekten – sprich schwul, schmutzig, schlecht, abartig – in die Welt des „vanilla sex" – heterosexuell, sauber, gut, möglichst heteronormativ – aufgestiegen ist[4], steht Billy im *Kondom des Grauens* nicht nur aufgrund seiner sittenwidrigen Berufswahl unter Tatverdacht: Eher steht er, gerade *weil* er homosexuell und MSM-Sexarbeiter ist, unter Generalverdacht.

Night fax from H.R. Giger, creative consultant for *Kondom des Grauens* (*Killer Condom*; 1996). Press material by Troma Entertainment for the film's US distribution.

of the "dick-biter" are up to mischief on the streets of New York, occasionally pouncing on innocent noses in the process.

In contrast to the crawling parasite creatures in body-horror gems such as David Cronenberg's *Shivers* (1975), which were invented to transform the world into an unrestrained orgy of repressed sexual energies, the beasts in this case were bred as ostensible condoms by the religious fanatic Dr. Riffleson (played by Iris Berben), with the help of a kidnapped genetic researcher in the catacombs of a hospital, to bring about her pronatalist world conspiracy against the vices of sodomy and "useless ejaculations." While in *Shivers*, the gradual fading of modern (white) embodiment is revealed as the transformation of ordered bodies into disordered bodies, or asexual bodies into hypersexual bodies,[6] Dr. Riffleson, in *Killer Condom*, could be seen as reversing this metamorphosis.

The rubber as a supposed threat to the church's biblical tenets simultaneously becomes a weapon against its actual beneficiaries, reflecting the zeitgeist that prevailed when the film (as well as the original comic) was first released: the AIDS crisis was at its peak. In 1989, as Sarah Schulman recalls in her oral history *Let the Record Show* (2021), seven thousand demonstrators joined ACT UP and WHAM! in front of St. Patrick's Cathedral on December 10 under the slogan "Stop the Church," disrupting a mass to protest the political influence of Cardinal John O'Connor and the Catholic Church in New York. In addition to condemning abortions and syringe exchanges, the church refused to distribute condoms, teach sex education in public schools, or provide information on safer sex methods, and it rejected the "Rainbow Curriculum," which promoted the inclusion of queer people and people of color in New York's public school curriculum.[7] German Curial Cardinal Ratzinger, who later became Pope Benedict XVI, was similarly a hard-liner who regularly sabotaged the fight against AIDS with "anti-condom" and homophobic messaging, which portrayed homosexuals as obstructing the divine world order.[8] In 2009, for example, the *pontifex maximus* stoked outrage in the media when he first addressed condom usage during his trip to Africa, claiming they would exacerbate the HIV crisis rather than solve it.[9] Meanwhile, Mackeroni preaches, "There aren't any condoms in heaven, nor any that bite."[10]

President Ronald Reagan, on the other hand, never uttered a word about condoms, let alone AIDS. He even prevented Charles Everett Koop, his surgeon general and then a leading figure in the anti-abortion movement, from informing the public about education strategies and the distribution of condoms,[11] at a time when up to thirty thousand Americans had already been diagnosed with the immunodeficiency syndrome (and countless more were infected with HIV).[12] Only the star appeal of Elizabeth Taylor could persuade Reagan to address the devastating AIDS crisis for the first time at a dinner organized by the American Foundation for AIDS Research in 1987.

An interpretation of *Killer Condom* as a parody of the ignorance of the growing AIDS crisis by a failing Reaganomics government, supported by the religious right, is epitomized by the Killer Condom attack on "For a Clean America" conservative presidential candidate Dick

Ein fataler Fehlglaube, wie sich herausstellt, denn das Killer-Kondom killt tatsächlich. Getarnt als Kondom, das heute wie ein „Snapchat-Logo"[5] daherkommt, kastriert es am liebsten penisbestückte Triebgesteuerte und Sexarbeiter*innen im Zimmer 308 des schäbigen Stundenhotels Quickies und findet in unverpackten Massenlieferungen von Gummies zum kleinen Preis Unterschlupf. Bald schon treiben Klone des „Pimmelbeißers" auf den Straßen New Yorks ihr Unwesen und erwischen dabei auch hin und wieder unschuldige Nasen.

Im Gegensatz zu den kriechenden Parasitenkreaturen in Body-Horror-Juwelen wie *Shivers* (1975) von David Cronenberg, die erfunden wurden, um die Welt in eine hemmungslose Orgie unterdrückter sexueller Energien zu transformieren, wurden die Bestien hier als vermeintliches Präservativ von einer religiös-fanatischen Iris Berben als Dr. Riffleson mit Hilfe eines gekidnappten Genforschers in den Katakomben eines Krankenhauses herangezüchtet – zur Verwirklichung ihrer pronatalistischen Weltverschwörung gegen sodomitische Laster und „nutzlose Ergüsse". Während sich in *Shivers* das allmähliche Schwinden einer modernen (weißen) Verkörperung als die Verwandlung von geordneten Körpern in ungeordnete Körper, asexuelle Körper in hypersexuelle Körper[6] offenbart, kehrt Dr. Riffleson diese Metamorphose in *Kondom des Grauens* gewissermaßen um.

Das Gummi als vermeintliche Bedrohung gegen den biblischen Wertekanon der Kirche wird hier gleichzeitig zur Waffe gegen seine eigentlichen Nutznießer*innen und spiegelt den vorherrschenden Zeitgeist während der Veröffentlichung des Films (beziehungsweise des Originalcomics) wider: Die Aidskrise war auf dem Peak. 1989 schlossen sich, wie sich etwa Sarah Schulman in ihrem Oral History-Buch *Let the Record Show* (2021) erinnert, am 10. Dezember unter dem Slogan „Stop the Church" 7.000 Demonstrant*innen ACT UP und WHAM! vor der St. Patrick's Cathedral an und störten eine Messe, um gegen den politischen Einfluss von Kardinal John O'Connor und der katholischen Kirche in New York zu protestieren. Neben Abtreibungen und Spritzentausch verweigerte die Kirche auch die Verteilung von Kondomen, den Sexualkundeunterricht an öffentlichen Schulen, die Aufklärung über Safer-Sex-Methoden sowie den „Regenbogenlehrplan", der damals die Einbeziehung von Queeren und People of Color in die Lehrpläne New Yorks vorsah.[7] Auch Kurienkardinal Ratzinger, der spätere Papst Benedikt XVI. sabotierte als Hardliner den Kampf gegen Aids regelmäßig mit „antikondomistischen" und homophoben Botschaften, nach denen Homosexuelle der göttlichen Ordnung der Welt in die Quere kämen.[8] 2009 stiftete der Pontifex maximus etwa auf seiner Afrikareise medial Empörung, als er sich erstmals zur Verwendung von Kondomen äußerte, die ihm zufolge das HIV-Problem verschlimmern würden, statt es zu lösen.[9] Unterdessen predigt Mackeroni: „Im Himmel gibt es keine Kondome und schon gar keine, die zubeißen."[10]

Präsident Ronald Reagan hingegen verlor in keinem Appell ein Wort über Kondome, geschweige denn über Aids, und hinderte sogar seinen Generalarzt und leitende Figur in der damaligen Anti-Abtreibungsbewegung,

McGouvern in the bathtub. Set to the soundtrack of *Jaws* (1975), the condom approaches on the back of a rubber duck like a great white shark stalking its prey; the "Dick" who has "had enough of scandals, drugs, and perversity"[13] is now "Dickless Dick," as a *New York Post* headline scandalously proclaims shortly afterwards.

Outside of the film, the emergence of HIV also caused scandals to break out behind the scenes of the Cold War, as Eastern and Western powers declared the virus a national security concern. In 1985, for example, Soviet biologists Jakob and Lilli Segal suspected that HIV had been created by genetic engineers in the U.S. Biological Weapons Institute in Fort Detrick, Maryland, at the behest of the Pentagon.[14] In a similar vein, the Killer Condom—hatched in a genetic laboratory by Russian professor Dr. Smirnoff as an unorthodox bioweapon substitute and deposited on the streets of New York by a Chinese spy (the object of Mackeroni's occasional xenophobic musings)—can ultimately get anyone, just like AIDS.

In contrast to this lab-created presidential penicide, however, AIDS primarily remained a private disaster, without a press conference, government action plan, or collective consternation. Ralf König's original comic, including the sequel *Down to the Bone* (*Bis auf die Knochen*; 1990), which was partly incorporated into the film script and partly discarded, also concerns deaths that escape the attention of the social majority. In the film, for example, we see nothing of the numerous bizarre murders in which homosexuals are devoured by an artificial creature named "Raoul," who then spits their bony remains out, leaving only squeaky-clean skeletons as traces for Mackeroni's investigations—emblematic "ghosts of public sex," as José Esteban Muñoz described the ghostly traces that circulate in former sites of gay cruising.[15]

Although in his comics, König only explicitly reflected on AIDS in his 1999 book *Super Paradies*, the "mourning" over the (AIDS) death of a scene is already mirrored in *Killer Condom*. From the early 1980s, this death was carried out by a criminalization campaign that was not only homophobic, but also classist and racist. AIDS's original names of GRID ("Gay-Related Immune Deficiency") and 4H Disease (after the four groups of people most affected: hemophiliacs, heroin users, Haitians, and homosexuals) are the corpus delicti. The opprobrium was also directed against the lifestyle of sexual promiscuity—indeed, against an entire liberated sexual culture that took place in public spaces.

AIDS ultimately revived the question of a culture of sexual opportunities. "Great anonymous sex," as had by John Giorno with an anonymous Keith Haring in the subway toilet on Prince Street in New York,[16] which Giorno recounts in his performance poetry book *You Got to Burn to Shine* (1992), now had to be rearticulated within an age of safe sex. This sparked heated debates, including in the gay scene in West Germany, about responsibility, the loss of sexual freedoms, and even "new gay morals," as activist and political scientist Andreas Salmen phrased it.[17] To campaign for the preservation of gay sexuality, writer Ronald Schernikau published his manifesto "Fickt Weiter!" ("Keep Fucking!") in the Berlin magazine *Siegessäule* in 1984:

Charles Everett Koop, daran, die Öffentlichkeit über Aufklärungsstrategien und die Verbreitung von Kondomen zu informieren[11], als bereits bis zu 30.000 US-Amerikaner*innen mit dem Immunschwächesyndrom diagnostiziert wurden (und unzählige mit HIV infiziert waren).[12] Erst der Starappeal einer Elizabeth Taylor konnte Reagan dazu bewegen, 1987 bei einem Abendessen der American Foundation for AIDS Research erstmals in einer Rede über die verheerende Aidslage zu sprechen.

Dass *Kondom des Grauens* hier auch als eine Parodie auf die Ignoranz der wachsenden Aidskrise seitens einer versagenden, ja von der religiösen Rechten gestützten Reaganomics-Regierung zu interpretieren ist, symbolisiert eine Attacke des Killer-Kondoms auf den konservativen „Für ein sauberes Amerika"-Präsidentschaftskandidaten Dick McGouvern in der Badewanne: Auf dem Rücken einer Gummiente schwimmt das Gummi zum Soundtrack von *Jaws* (1975) wie der weiße Hai an seine Beute heran: Der „Dick", der „genug von Skandalen und Perversitäten hat"[13], ist nun „Dickless Dick", wie es kurz darauf eine Schlagzeile in der *New York Post* skandalisiert.

Auch jenseits des Films skandalisierte man während des Aufkommens von HIV hinter den Kulissen des Kalten Kriegs, wo Ost- und Westmächte den Virus zum nationalen Sicherheitsanliegen erklärten. So vermuteten etwa die sowjetischen Biologen Jakob und Lilli Segal 1985, dass HIV auf Drängen des Pentagons im U.S. Biological Weapons Institute in Fort Detrick, Maryland, durch Geningenieure erschaffen wurde.[14] Auch das im Genlabor vom russischen Professor Dr. Smirnoff ausgebrütete Killer Kondom als unorthodoxer Biowaffenersatz, das ein chinesischer Spion (über den Mackeroni selbst hin und wieder fremdenfeindlich mutmaßt) in den Straßen New Yorks deponiert, kann letztendlich jeden erwischen – ebenso wie Aids.

Im Gegensatz zum Penismord der Laborkreation am Präsidenten blieb Aids jedoch vornehmlich ein privates Desaster ohne Pressekonferenz, staatlichen Maßnahmenplan und kollektiver Betroffenheit. Jenes Sterben jenseits des mehrheitsgesellschaftlichen Interesses thematisiert auch Ralf König in seinem Originalcomic, der die Fortsetzung *Bis auf die Knochen* (1990) umfasst, die für das Drehbuch zum Film teils verarbeitet, aber auch teils verworfen wurde. So sieht man im Film nichts von der Reihe bizarrer Morde, bei denen Homosexuelle von einer künstlichen Kreatur namens Raoul verschlungen und ihre knöchernen Überreste ausgespuckt werden, die nur noch blitzsaubere Skelette als Spur für Mackeronis Ermittlungen hinterlässt – sinnbildliche „Geister des öffentlichen Sex"[15], wie sie José Esteban Muñoz nannte.

Auch wenn König erst in seinem 1999 veröffentlichten Buch *Super Paradies* offiziell in seinen Comics über das Thema Aids reflektierte, spiegelt sich bereits in *Kondom des Grauens* das „Mourning" über den (Aids-)Tod einer Szene. Dazu zählte seit Anfang der 1980er Jahre eine nicht nur homophobe, sondern zugleich klassistische und rassistische Kriminalisierungskampagne. Die ursprüngliche Bezeichnung von Aids als GRID für „Gay-Related Immune Deficiency" und „4H Disease" nach den vier am stärksten betroffenen Personengruppen, Hämophile, Heroinkonsument*innen, Haitianer*innen und Homosexuelle sind Corpus Delicti

Elisa R. Linn

"and more clearly 'the decision to choose monogamy for sexual fidelity should certainly not be made solely out of fear of AIDS or other diseases.' That's it. ... in plain language: If you stop fucking now, you should stop smoking drinking eating working driving cars using spray paint plastic radios cinemas people."[18]

As early as 1985, Ralf König had already illustrated comics that advocated for safer sex, such as *Der Verhüter* (*The Contracepter*) for the German AIDS Service Organization, which showed his iconic bulbous-nosed characters masturbating or having anal sex with a condom.[19] However, the flippant Killer Condom with bared teeth also reflects the perceived off-putting sternness of clean safer sex and the fear that the gay movement would be largely subjected to the straight knife in real life. Ironically, protests such as "Stop the Church"—in the eyes of Sarah Schulman—also made the future assimilationist agenda of a gay rights movement acceptable *in* and not in front of the church for the first time, as they upheld natalism, the nuclear family, monogamy, and marriage. This ultimately paved the way for homonormativity (Lisa Duggan) and later homonationalism (Jasbir Puar): a facet of modernity and a historical shift marked by the perception of (some) homosexual bodies as worthy of protection by nation-states, a constitutive and fundamental reorientation of the relationship between the state, capitalism, and sexuality.[20]

Leo Bersani has likewise argued that the continuous politicization of sex could be the result of the desire to purify sex of its own negativity, which would be tantamount to a desexualization of sex.[21] And yet: "NO GLOVE, NO LOVE and DON'T BALK AT SAFER SEX."[22]

In his book *Die Kapsel* (*The Capsule*; 2018) Martin Reichert states that even healthcare scientists such as Rolf Rosenbrock did not believe the "zero risk" provided by abstinence or phone sex to be a satisfactory substitute during the AIDS crisis, as they "reduce the sexual act to the dimension of a kind of mechanical relaxation."[23] Instead, Rosenbrock's book *AIDS kann schneller besiegt werden* (*AIDS Can Be Beaten More Quickly*; 1986) promoted the use of condoms and lifestyle changes in collaboration with those affected, rather than complicated "checklists with up to sixteen sex techniques."[24]

Thus, safer sex practices ultimately allowed for an escape from abstinence and to a coupled binary gender system, which was largely propagated and seen as respectable by most media—a fact meticulously demonstrated in *Killer Condom*. Here, the use of condoms is taken for granted, such as the warning Mackeroni gives his visibly anxious straight cop partner Sam, clad in a leather harness and choker, before his undercover mission in a gay club: "Be careful who you have sex with and always check the condom first."[25]

And finally, "Loogi," as Mackeroni is affectionately called by transgender sex worker Babette (and former cop Bob) after she fell for him following a one-night stand, is forced to constantly demand tolerance from those around him, given the omnipresent discriminatory "compulsory heterosexuality."[26] At the same time that he chases the Killer Condom, Mackeroni must endlessly rebel against repressive educational practices—including his own. He

davon. Dabei richtete sich die Hetze auch gegen den Lebensstil jener, die sexuelle Promiskuität, ja eine sich im öffentlichen Raum manifestierende freie sexuelle Kultur praktizierten.

Mit Aids stellte sich somit letztlich die Frage nach einer Kultur der sexuellen Möglichkeiten neu. „Great Anonymous Sex", wie ihn etwa John Giorno mit einem anonymen Keith Haring auf der U-Bahn-Toilette der Prince Street in New York hatte[16], wie Giorno es in seinem Performance-Poetry-Band *You Got to Burn to Shine* (1992) schilderte, musste fortan ins Zeitalter des Safer Sex übersetzt werden. Es entfachten hitzige Debatten, auch in der Schwulenszene in Westdeutschland, um Verantwortung, den Verlust sexueller Freiheiten oder gar einer „neuen schwulen Moral"[17], wie es der Aktivist und Politologe Andreas Salmen formulierte. Um sich für eine Bewahrung schwuler Sexualität stark zu machen, veröffentlichte auch der Schriftsteller Ronald Schernikau 1984 sein Manifest unter dem Titel „Fickt Weiter!" im Stadtmagazin Siegessäule: „[...] und deutlicher, die entscheidung zur monogamie für sexuelle treue, sollte sicher nicht allein aus angst vor aids oder anderen erkrankungen getroffen werden.' that's it. [...] mal ganz im klartext: wer jetzt aufhört zu ficken, sollte aufhörn zu rauchen trinken essen arbeiten autofahrn spraydosen benutzen lackfarbe plastik radios kinos menschen."[18]

Während Ralf König für die Aidshilfe bereits 1985 Safer-Sex-Comics wie *Der Verhüter* mit seinen ikonischen Knollnasenfiguren zur Aufklärung illustrierte, die sie beim Onanieren oder beim Analsex mit Kondom zeigen[19], spiegelt sich im flachsinnig daherkommenden Killer-Kondom mit fletschenden Zähnen auch die real wahrgenommene lusthemmende Strenge des sauberen Safer Sex wider und die Befürchtung, inwiefern die Schwulenbewegung ans Hetero-Messer geliefert werden würde. Ironischerweise machten auch Proteste wie Stop the Church zum ersten Mal *in* und nicht vor der Kirche – in den Augen von Sarah Schulman – damals schon die künftige assimilatorische Agenda einer Schwulenrechtsbewegung schmackhaft, die den Pronatalismus, die Kernfamilie, die Monogamie und die Ehe hochhält und letztlich den Weg für Homonormativität (Lisa Duggan) bis hin zum Homonationalismus (Jasbir Puar) ebnete[20]: eine Facette der Moderne und ein historischer Wandel, der durch den Eintritt *einiger* homosexueller Körper in die Schutzwürdigkeit des Nationalstaats geprägt ist und damit die Beziehung zwischen Staat, Kapitalismus und Sexualität neu orchestriere.[21] Dass die fortschreitende Politisierung von Sex das Ergebnis des Wunsches sein kann, Sex von seiner eigenen Negativität zu reinigen, was einer Entsexualisierung des Sex gleichkomme, bemerkte auch Leo Bersani.[22] Und dennoch:„NO GLOVE, NO LOVE and DON'T BALK AT SAFER SEX."[23]

Martin Reichert beschreibt in *Die Kapsel* (2018), dass auch Gesundheitswissenschaftler wie Rolf Rosenbrock während der Aidskrise nicht an ein „Null-Risiko" durch Enthaltsamkeit oder Telefonsex als Substitutbefriedigung glaubten, die „den Geschlechtsakt auf Dimension einer Art mechanischer Entspannung reduzieren."[24] Stattdessen zielte Rosenbrock mit seinem Buch *AIDS kann schneller besiegt werden* (1986) auf die Nutzung von Kondomen und Verhaltensveränderung in Kooperation mit Betroffenen

On the set of *Killer Condom* (1996).

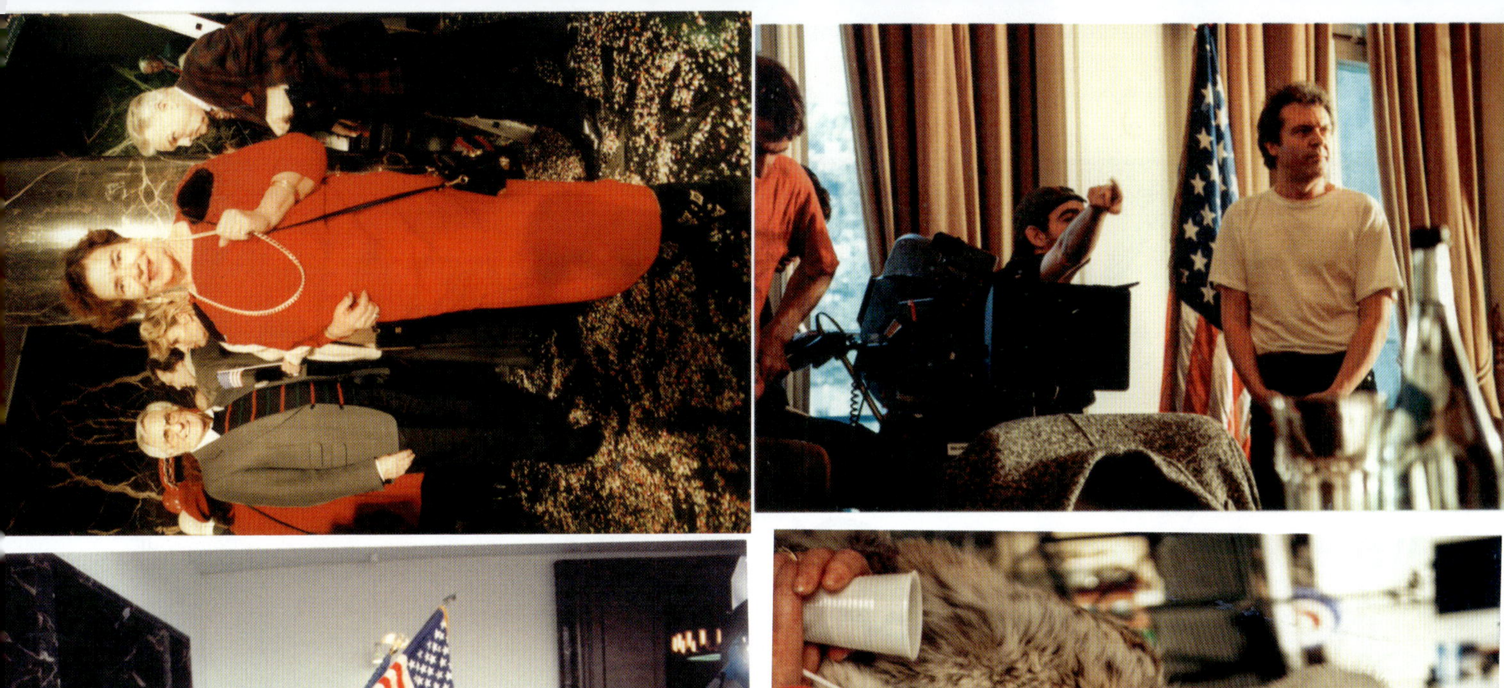
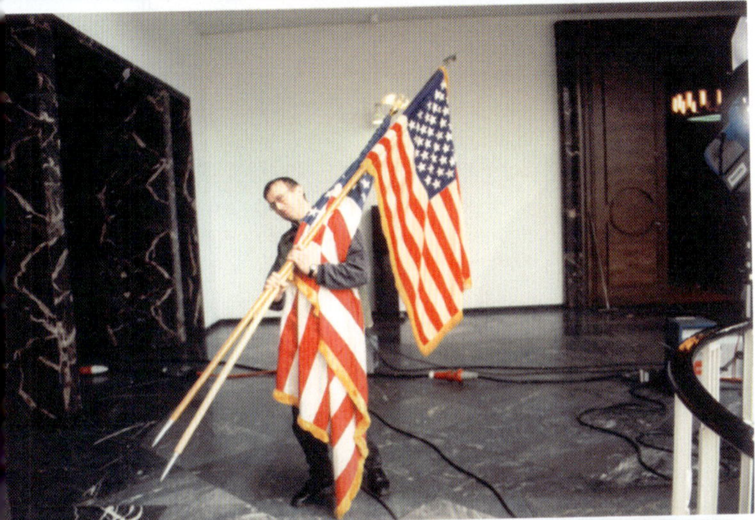
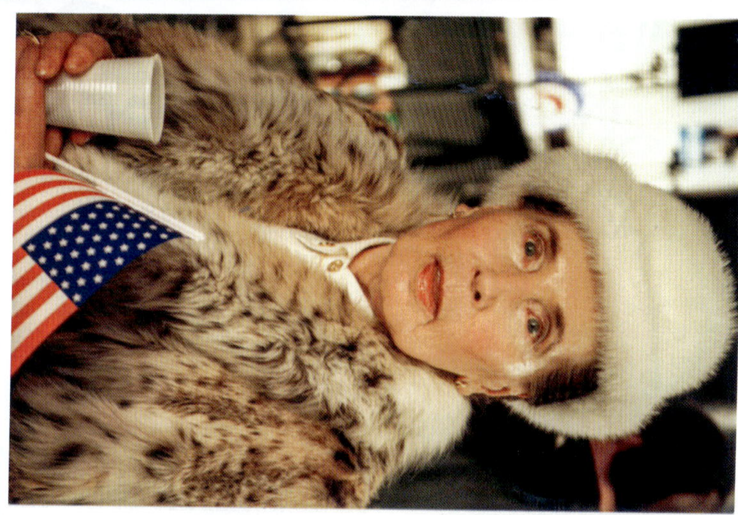
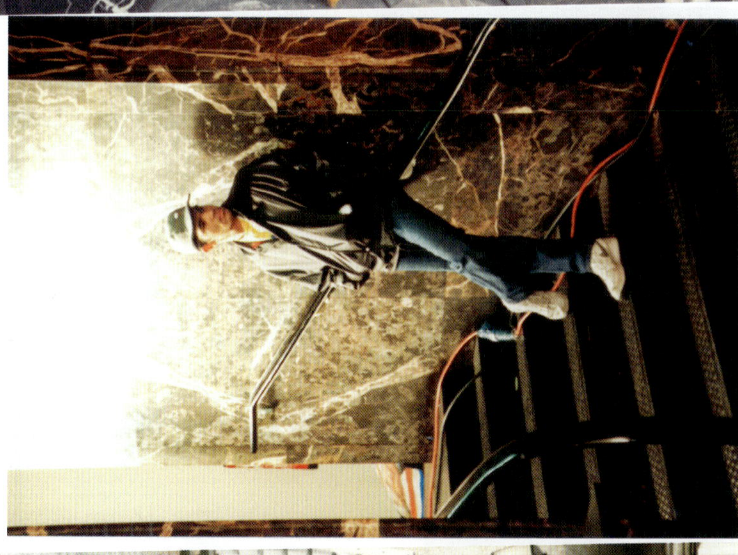
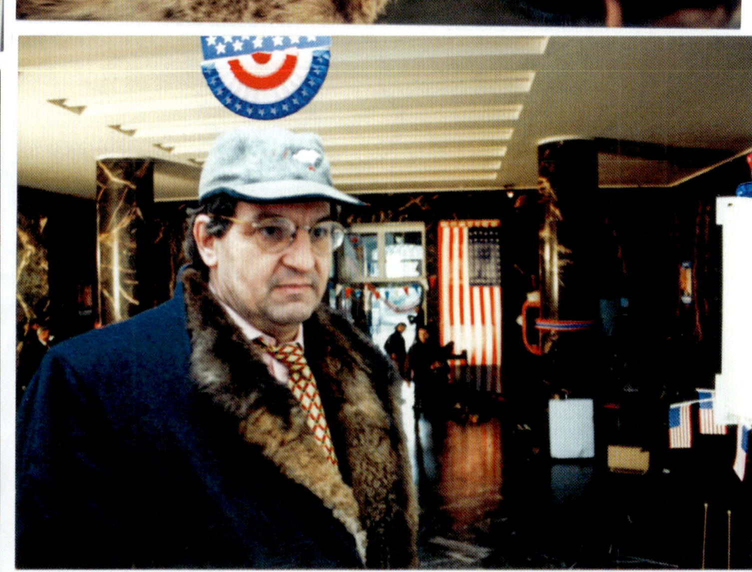
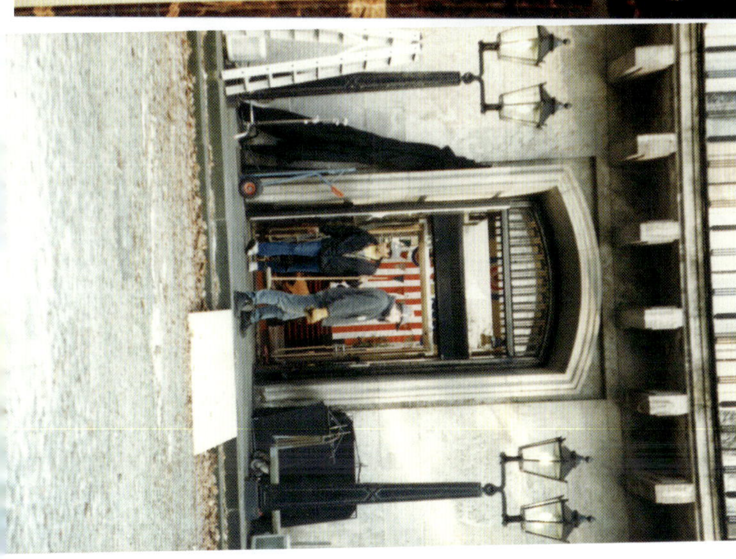
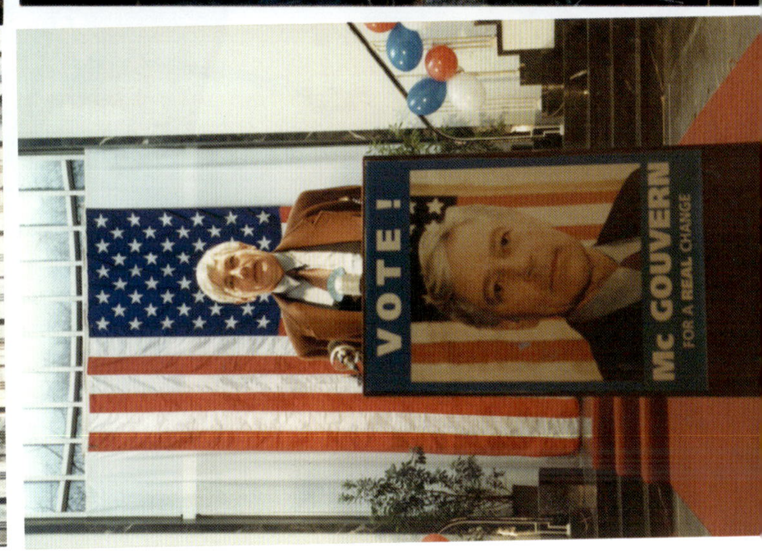
VOTE!
MC GOUVERN
FOR A REAL CHANGE

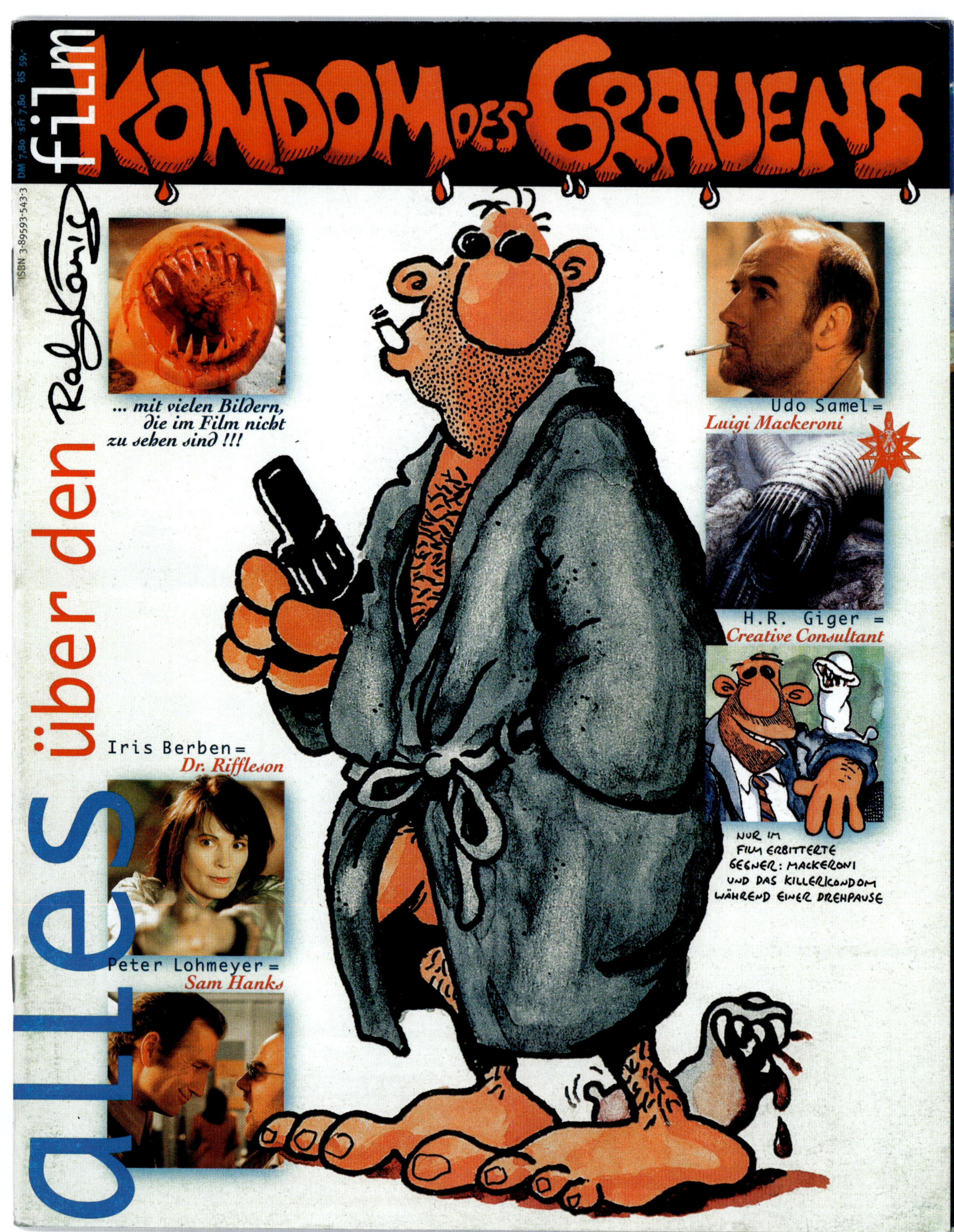

Press material for *Killer Condom* (1996).

11

frequently and ignorantly calls Babette "Bob," even transphobically threatening to "squeeze the artificial hormones out of those pathetic tits" after Babette calls him a "little Sicilian faggot." [27] Babette, played in the film by Leonard Lansink, who otherwise portrays meaty straight detectives on German television, indicates the impact the AIDS crisis had not only on communities on the margins of society, but also on the construction of identity itself, as it undermined any understanding of the self and subjectivity as something "whole, untouchable, inviolable, and definable." [28]

Even before the onslaught of the epidemic and the subsequent reactionary political climate, which seriously altered the development of the gay movement in the 1980s from the emancipatory liberation of the Stonewall Riots in 1969, Mario Mieli used the term "edu-castration" to describe educational measures that enforced monosexuality and the eradication of poly-erotic tendencies. According to Mieli, who committed suicide in 1983, these repressed desires produced malformed bodies and unhappy subjects—which he saw as originating within the church and persisting under capitalism. [29] In this context, homosexual desire could tip over into homophobic contempt with the advent of the AIDS crisis, which caused sex to be inextricably tied to the pressure of mortality: "Heterosexual males also fear the excremental aura of anal intercourse. 'But Love has pitched his mansion in / The place of excrement' (Yeats)." [30]

"It's my job to rummage deep down in the dirt," [31] Mackeroni monologues in melancholic street scenes to nineties Eurodance and Sicilian music strumming from off-screen, evoking that universal feeling of loneliness of a different kind of Scorsesian taxi driver: "I don't kid myself about love anymore. What is love? It all boils down to sex anyway." [32]

jenseits komplizierter „Check-Listen mit bis zu 16 Sex-Techniken." [25]

Somit ermöglichten Safer-Sex-Praktiken letztendlich eben gerade der Abstinenz bis zur monogamen Zweipaargeschlechtlichkeit zu entkommen, die von den meisten Medien damals propagiert wurden und als respektabel galten, was *Kondom des Grauens* beinahe penibel demonstriert. Hier wird immerzu selbstverständlich vom Gebrauch des Kondoms gesprochen, wenn Mackeroni etwa seinen sichtlich verängstlichten Hetero-Cop-Kollegen Sam mit Leder-Harness und Choker vor seiner Undercover-Mission im Schwulenclub warnt: „Du solltest lieber aufpassen, wenn du mit jemanden Sex machst und vorher das Kondom genau untersuchen." [26]

Schließlich muss „Loogi", wie Mackeroni liebevoll von der transgender Sexarbeiterin Babette (dem Ex-Cop Bob) genannt wird, nachdem sie ihm nach einem One-Night-Stand verfiel, sich angesichts einer omnipräsenten diskriminierenden „Zwangsheterosexualität" [27] von seinem Umfeld in *Kondom des Grauens* immer wieder Toleranz einfordern. Während er das Killer-Kondom jagt, muss Mackeroni immerzu gegen repressive Erziehungsprozesse rebellieren – seine eigenen mit eingeschlossen. So nennt er doch Babette ignoranterweise immerzu „Bob" und droht ihr in transphober Manier sogar, nachdem Babette ihn als „kleine sizilianische Tunte" bezeichnet, ihr „die künstlichen Hormone aus [ihren] lächerlichen Titten zu quetschen." [28] Dabei versinnbildlicht Babette im Film, hier gespielt durch Leonard Lansink, der sonst den kernigen Hetero-Kriminalkommissar im Deutschen Fernsehen gibt, welche Auswirkungen die Aidskrise nicht nur auf Gemeinschaften am Rande der Gesellschaft, sondern auch auf die Konstruktion von Identität an sich hatte: Sie untergrub jegliches Verständnis des Selbst und der Subjektivität als „ganz, unantastbar, unverletzlich und definierbar" [29].

Noch vor dem Ansturm der Epidemie und eines reaktionären politischen Klimas, das die Entwicklung der Schwulenbewegung in den 80er Jahren nach dem emanzipatorischen Befreiungsschlag des Stonewall-Aufstands 1969 gravierend veränderte, umschrieb Mario Mieli mit „Edukastration" Erziehungsmaßnahmen, die zur Monosexualität und zur Auslöschung polyerotischer Tendenzen zwinge. Mieli zufolge, der 1983 Suizid beging, brächten diese unterdrückten Wünsche missgestaltete Körper und unglückliche Subjekte hervor – was mit der Kirche beginne und sich im Kapitalismus fortsetze. [30] Hierbei konnte homosexuelles Begehren auch mit Aufkommen der Aidskrise, die fortan Sex an den Druck der Sterblichkeit fesselte, schon einmal in homophobe Verachtung umkippen: „Heterosexual males also fear the excremental aura of anal intercourse. 'But Love has pitched his mansion in/The place of excrement' (Yeats)." [31]

„Mein Job ist es, ganz tief unten in der Scheiße zu wühlen" [32], monologisiert Mackeroni unterdessen in melancholischen Straßenszenen zu 90er-Eurodance und sizilianischer Klimpermusik aus dem Off, was das universelle Gefühl von Einsamkeit eines entfremdeten Scorsesian *Taxi Drivers* der anderen Art heraufbeschwört: „Ich mache mir keine Illusionen mehr was Liebe angeht. Was ist schon Liebe? Letztlich dreht sich doch alles nur um Sex." [33]

Elisa R. Linn

1   This is how film critic B. Ruby Rich described New Queer Cinema in 2004, which has been a feature of the film festival circuit since the early 1990s: "Something new, renegotiating subjectivities, annexing whole genres, revising histories in their image." Cf. B. Ruby Rich, "New Queer Cinema," in *New Queer Cinema: A Critical Reader*, ed. Michele Aaron (Edinburgh: Edinburgh University Press, 2004), 15–16.
2   *Killer Condom*, directed by Martin Waltz (1996, Germany; 2024, DVD, Vinegar Syndrome) (translated by Lisa Contag).
3   Cf. Victor Minichiello and John Scott, eds., introduction to *Male Sex Work and Society* (New York: Columbia University Press, 2014).
4   Cf. ibid., 64.
5   Shane Wilson, "It Came From the Reader-Suggested Queue: 'Killer Condom' (1996)," 366 Weird Movies, August 29, 2023, https://366weirdmovies.com/it-came-from-the-reader-suggested-queue-killer-condom-1996/.
6   Cf. Jo Eadie, "Embodied politics and extreme disgust: an investigation into the meanings of bodily order and bodily disorder, with particular reference to the work of William Burroughs and David Cronenberg" (PhD diss., University of Nottingham, 1998).
7   Cf. Sarah Schulman, *Let the Record Show: A Political History of ACT UP New York, 1987–1993* (New York: Farrar, Straus and Giroux, 2021), 138.
8   Cf. Henning Tümmers, *AIDS: Autopsie einer Bedrohung im geteilten Deutschland* (Göttingen: Wallstein Verlag, 2017), 161.
9   "Papst empört Kritiker mit Kondom-Verbot," *Spiegel Online*, March 18, 2009, https://www.spiegel.de/panorama/gesellschaft/benedikt-reise-papst-empoert-kritiker-mit-kondom-verbot-a-613964.html.
10   Cf. *Killer Condom*.
11   Cf. Craig A. Rimmerman, *From Identity to Politics" The Lesbian and Gay Movements in the United States* (Philadelphia: Temple University Press, 2002), 88.
12   Cf. Seth Kalichman, *Denying Aids: Conspiracy Theories, Pseudoscience, and Human Tragedy* (New York: Copernicus, 2019), 120.
13   Cf. *Killer Condom*.
14   Cf. Erhard Geißler, "'Lieber AIDS als gar nichts aus dem Westen!' Wie Partei- und Staatsführung der DDR mit dem AIDS-Problem umgingen," *Zeitschrift des Forschungsverbund SED-Staat* 22, 2007, 98.
15   Cf. José Esteban Muñoz, *Cruising Utopia: The Then and There of Queer Futurity* (New York: New York University Press, 2009), p. 362.
16   Cf. ibid., p. 358 et seq.
17   Andreas Salmen, "Endlich aus der Opfer-Rolle herauskommen," *Rosa Flieder* 63, 1987, 12–13 (translated by Lisa Contag).
18   Ronald M. Schernikau, "Fickt Weiter!", *Siegessäule*, no. 11, 1984, 27 (translated by Lisa Contag).
19   Cf. Martin Reichert, *Die Kapsel. Aids in der Bundesrepublik* (Berlin: Suhrkamp Verlag, 2018), 70–71.
20   Jasbir Puar, "Rethinking Homonationalism," *International Journal of Middle East Studies* 45, no. 2, 2013, 337.
21   Cf. Leo Bersani, *Is the Rectum a Grave? And Other Essays* (Chicago: University of Chicago Press, 2010).

1   Die Filmkritikerin B. Ruby Rich beschrieb 2004 so das New Queer Cinema, das ab den frühen 1990er Jahren in der Festivalfilmszene eine Rolle zu spielen begann: „something new, renegotiating subjectivities, annexing whole genres, revising histories in their image." Vgl. B. Ruby Rich, „New Queer Cinema", in: *New Queer Cinema: A Critical Reader*, hrsg. von Michele Aaron, Edinburgh 2004, S. 15–16.
2   Martin Waltz (Regisseur), *Kondom des Grauens* [Film], Deutschland 1996.
3   Vgl. Victor Minichiello, John Scott, *Male Sex Work and Society*, New York 2014, Einleitung.
4   Vgl. ebd., S. 64.
5   Shane Wilson, „It Came From the Reader-Suggested Queue: Killer Condom (1996)", in: 366 Weird Movies, 29.08.2023, https://366weirdmovies.com/it-came-from-the-reader-suggested-queue-killer-condom-1996/ (letzter Zugriff: 13.04.2024).
6   Vgl. Jo Eadie, *Embodied politics and extreme disgust: an investigation into the meanings of bodily order and bodily disorder, with particular reference to the work of William Burroughs and David Cronenberg*. Diss. University of Nottingham 1998.
7   Vgl. Sarah Schulman, *Let the Record Show: A Political History of ACT UP New York, 1987–1993*, New York 2021, S. 138 (Kindle-Version).
8   Vgl. Henning Tümmers, *AIDS: Autopsie einer Bedrohung im geteilten Deutschland*, Göttingen 2017, S. 161.
9   „Papst empört Kritiker mit Kondom-Verbot", in: *Spiegel Online*, 18.03.2009, https://www.spiegel.de/panorama/gesellschaft/benedikt-reise-papst-empoert-kritiker-mit-kondom-verbot-a-613964.html (letzter Zugriff: 18.04.2024).
10   Vgl. *Kondom des Grauens* (wie Anm. 2).
11   Vgl. Craig A. Rimmerman, *From Identity to Politics. The Lesbian and Gay Movement in the United States*, Philadelphia 2002, S. 88.
12   Vgl. Seth Kalichman, *Denying Aids: Conspiracy Theories, Pseudoscience, and Human Tragedy*, New York 2019, S. 120.
13   Vgl. *Kondom des Grauens* (wie Anm. 2).
14   Vgl. Erhard Geißler, „'Lieber AIDS als gar nichts aus dem Westen!' Wie Partei- und Staatsführung der DDR mit dem AIDS-Problem umgingen", in: *Zeitschrift des Forschungsverbund SED-Staat*, Heft 22, 2007, S. 91–116, hier 98.
15   Vgl. José Esteban Muñoz, *Cruising Utopia: The Then and There of Queer Futurity*, New York 2009.
16   Vgl. ebd., S. 358 ff.
17   Andreas Salmen, „Endlich aus der Opfer-Rolle herauskommen", in: *Rosa Flieder*, Heft 63, 1987, S. 12–13. Vgl. Adrian Lehne und Veronika Springmann, „Promiske Sexualität oder monogame Beziehung? Freiheit, Moral und Verantwortung in der westdeutschen Homosexuellenbewegung", in: *WerkstattGeschichte*, Heft 84, 2021, S. 79 ff.
18   Ronald M. Schernikau, „Fickt Weiter!", in: *Siegessäule* 11 (1984), S. 27.
19   Vgl. Martin Reichert, *Die Kapsel. Aids in der Bundesrepublik*, Berlin 2018, S. 70–71.

22   The slogan adorned the banners of a 1988 protest at Shea Stadium in New York organized by the NY ACT UP Women's Caucus, which also protested against the misconception that heterosexual women supposedly could not contract AIDS. Cf. Maxime Wolf, "MAKE IT WORK FOR YOU: Academia and Political Organizing in Lesbian and Gay Communities," https://actupny.org/documents/academia.html (last accessed April 14, 2024).
23   Rolf Rosenbrock, *Aids kann schneller besiegt werden. Gesundheitspolitik am Beispiel einer Infektionskrankheit* (Hamburg: VSA-Verlag, 1986), 45 (translated by Lisa Contag).
24   Ibid. (translated by Lisa Contag).
25   Cf. *Killer Condom.*
26   Cf. Adrienne Rich, "Compulsory Heterosexuality and Lesbian Existence," *Signs: Journal of Women in Culture and Society* 5, no. 4, 1980.
27   Cf. *Killer Condom.*
28   Monica Pearl, "AIDS and New Queer Cinema," in *New Queer Cinema: A Critical Reader*, ed. Michele Aaron (Edinburgh: Edinburgh University Press, 2004), 24.
29   Cf. Mario Mieli, *Towards a Gay Communism: Elements of a Homosexual Critique* (London: Pluto Press, 2018).
30   Ibid., 149.
31   Cf. *Killer Condom.*
32   Ibid.

20   Vgl. Sarah Schulman (wie Anm. 7), S. 139.
21   Jasbir Puar, „Rethinking Homonationalism", in: *International Journal of Middle East Studies*, Band 45, Nr. 2, 2013, S. 337. Von der Autorin aus dem Englischen ins Deutsche übersetzt.
22   Vgl. Leo Bersani, *Is the Rectum a Grave? And Other Essays*, Chicago and London 2010.
23   Der Slogan zierte 1988 die Banner einer Protestaktion im Shea Stadium in New York, die von der NY ACT UP Women's Causus organisiert wurde, welche auch gegen den Irrglauben protestierte, dass heterosexuelle Frauen angeblich kein Aids bekommen könnten. Siehe Maxime Wolf, „MAKE IT WORK FOR YOU: Academia and Political Organizing in Lesbian and Gay Communities", https://actupny.org/documents/academia.html (letzter Zugriff: 14.04.2024).
24   Rolf Rosenbrock, *Aids kann schneller besiegt werden. Gesundheitspolitik am Beispiel einer Infektionskrankheit*, Hamburg 1986, S. 45.
25   Ebd.
26   Vgl. *Kondom des Grauens* (wie Anm. 2).
27   Vgl. Adrienne Rich, „Compulsory Heterosexuality and Lesbian Existence", in: *Signs: Journal of Women in Culture and Society*, Band 5, Nr. 4, 1980, S. 631–660.
28   Vgl. *Kondom des Grauens* (wie Anm. 2).
29   Monica Pearl, „AIDS and New Queer Cinema", in: Aaron (wie Anm. 1), S. 24.
30   Vgl. Mario Mieli, *Towards a Gay Communism: Elements of a Homosexual Critique* (1977), London 2018.
31   Ebd., S. 149.
32   Vgl. *Kondom des Grauens* (wie Anm. 2).
33   Ebd.

Elisa R. Linn (Elisa Linn Roguszczak) is a writer, exhibition maker, educator, and Whitney ISP graduate based in Lüneburg. She codirects the Halle für Kunst Lüneburg e.V. and teaches at Leuphana University and ZHdK (Zürcher Hochschule der Künste). Her PhD under the supervision of Marina Gržinić and forthcoming book look at how the Berlin Wall functioned as a condom against the Other during the AIDS crisis and amidst the Cold War confrontation.

Film (Fluentum)

Reel 1
14 - 25 September 2021

010   Medium Yellow
013   Straw Tint
019   Fire
027   Medium Red
036   Medium Pink
049   Medium Purple
061   Mist Blue
079   Just Blue
088   Lime Green

Film (Fluentum)

Reel 2
1 - 23 October 2021

089   Moss Green
101   Yellow
103   Straw
106   Primary Red
115   Peacock Blue
116   Medium Blue-Green
117   Steel Blue
124   Dark Green
132   Medium Blue

Margaret Honda, Scores for *Film (Fluentum)*, 2021.
Included in the exhibition *Time Without End*, Fluentum, Berlin, 2021.

Film (Fluentum)

Reel 3
29 October - 20 November 2021

139	Primary Green
147	Apricot
152	Pale Gold
156	Chocolate
161	Slate Blue
162	Bastard Amber
170	Deep Lavender
181	Congo Blue
242	Fluorescent 4300 Kelvin

Film (Fluentum)

Reel 4
6 November - 11 December 2021

328   Follies Pink
650   Industrial Vapor
651   Hi Sodium
652   Urban Vapor
728   Steel Green
2005 VS Cyan
2009 VS Violet

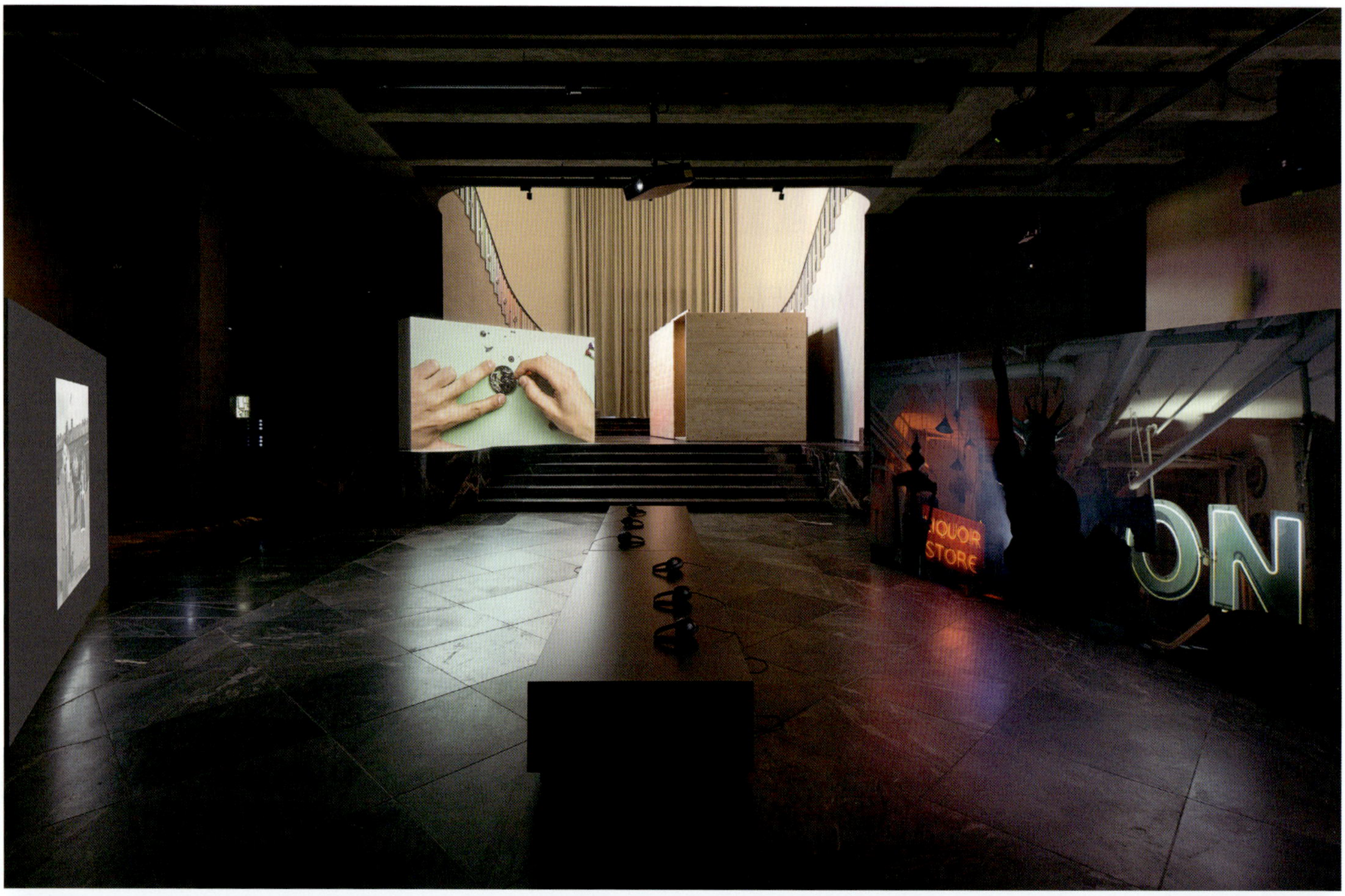

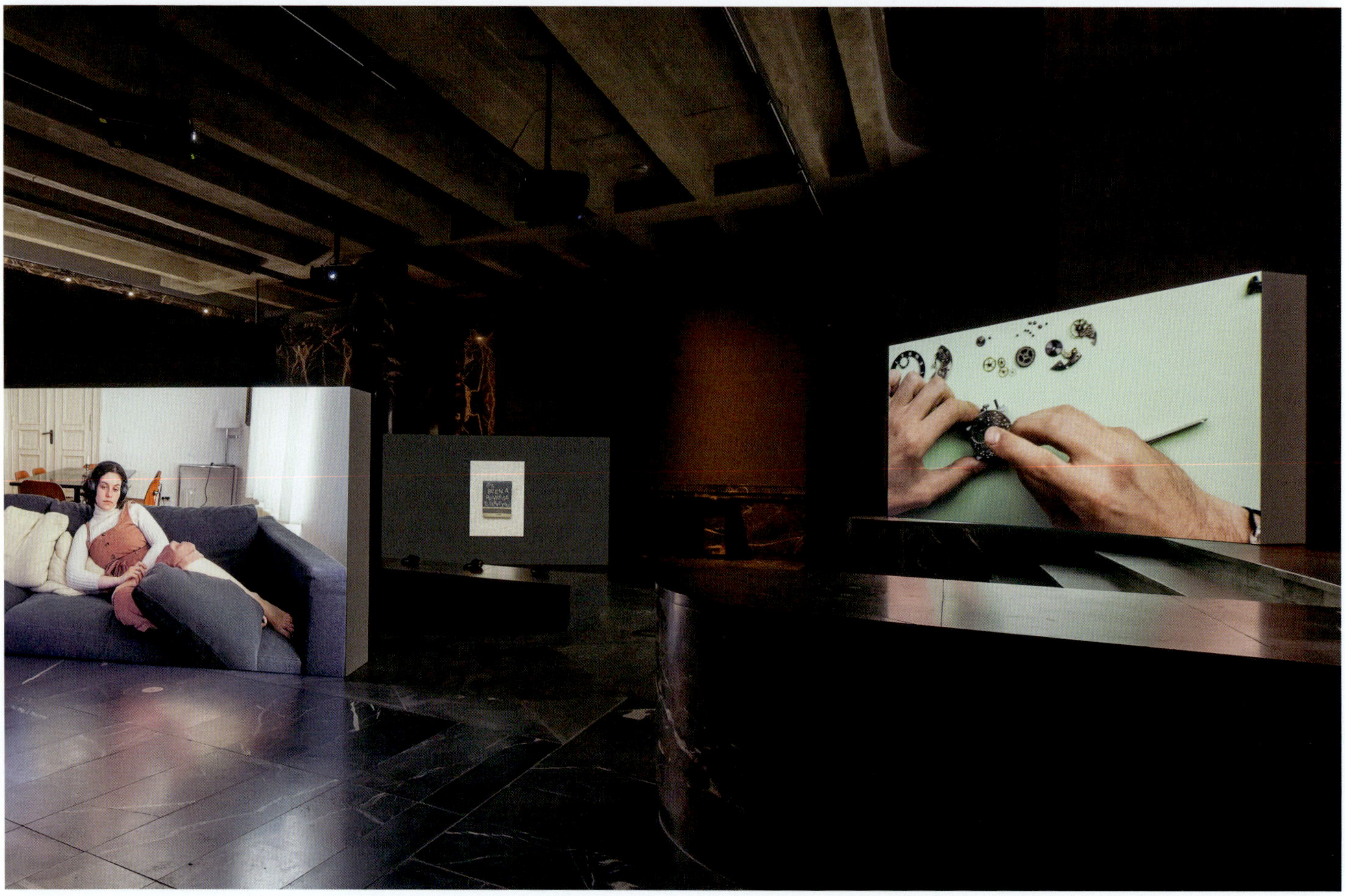

Installation views of the group exhibition *Time Without End*, Fluentum, Berlin, 2021.

With works by 13BC (Vic Brooks, Evan Calder Williams, Lucy Raven), Klaus vom Bruch, Keren Cytter,

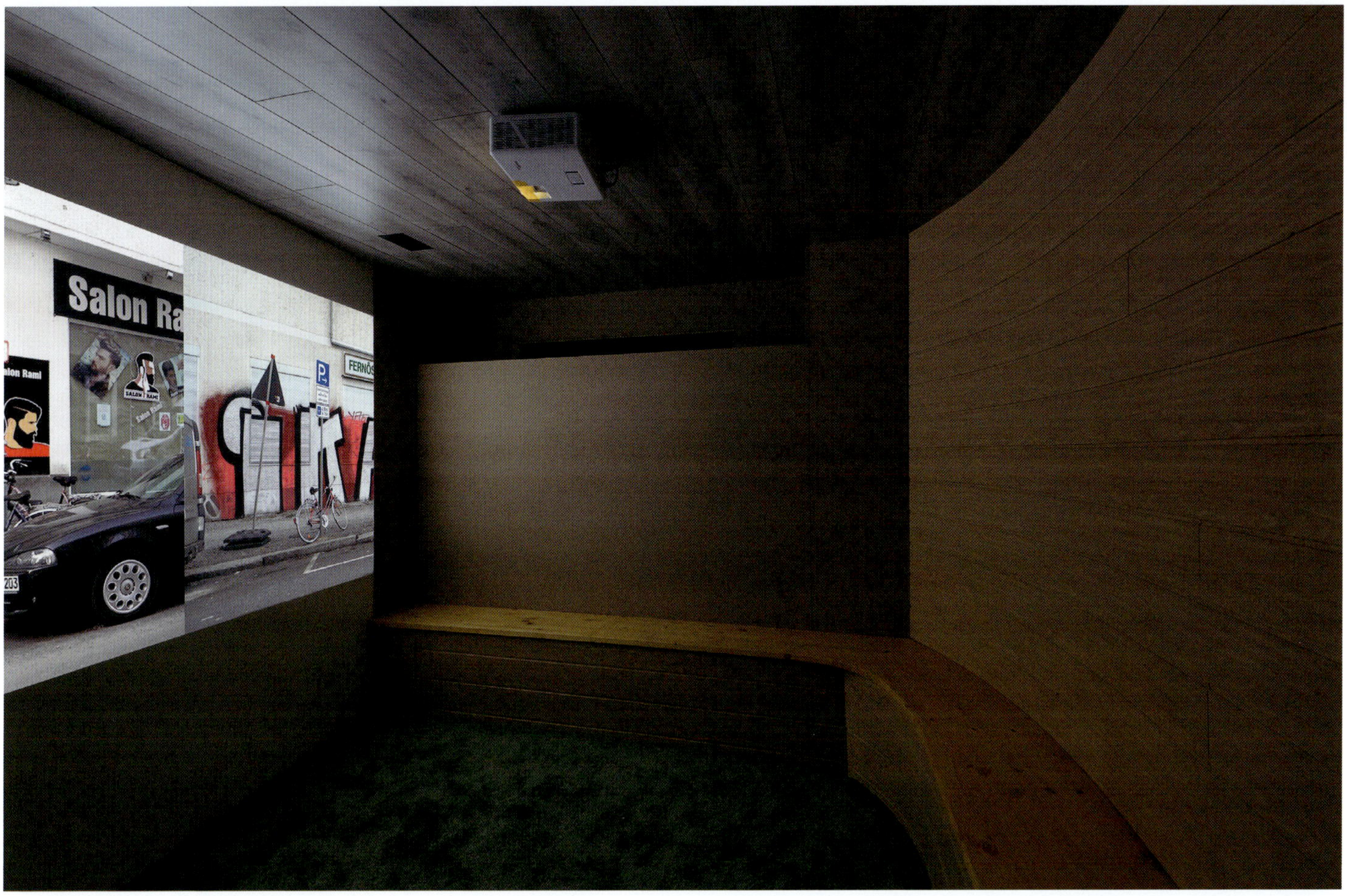

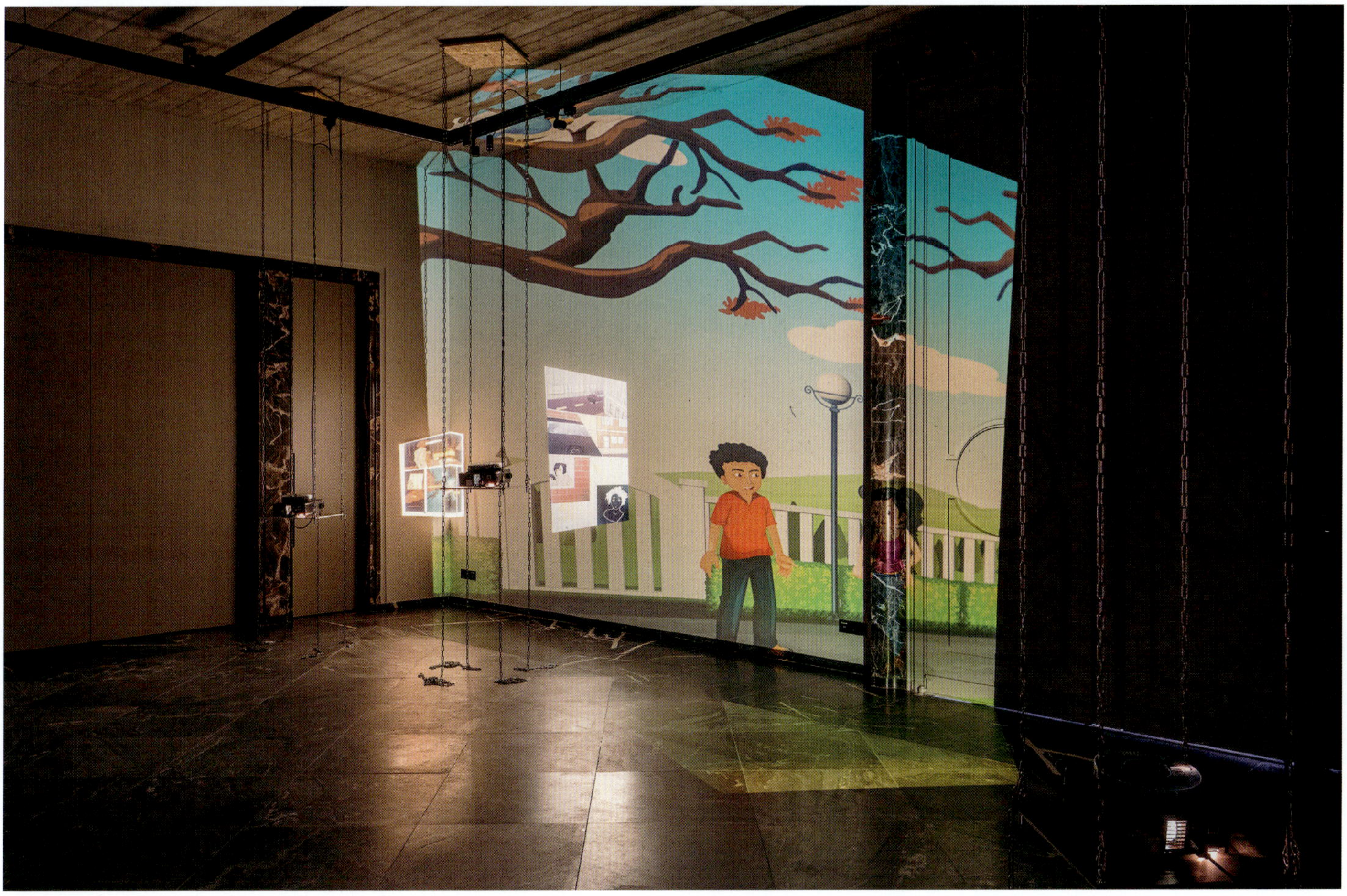

Loretta Fahrenholz, Margaret Honda, D'Ette Nogle,
Richard Sides, Valerie Snobeck, Florian Wüst.

Part of the program series
In Medias Res: Media, (Still) Moving, 2021–24.

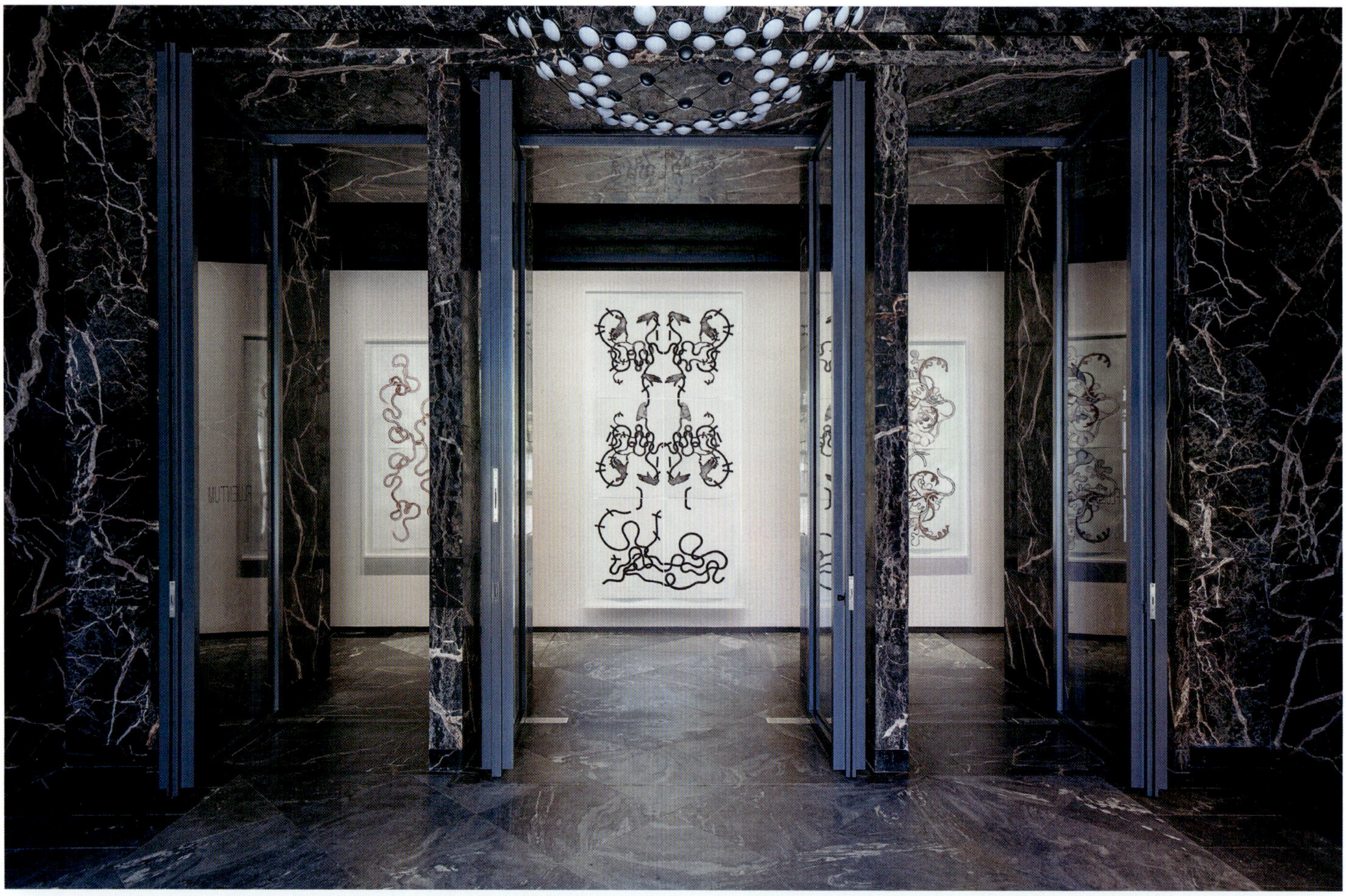

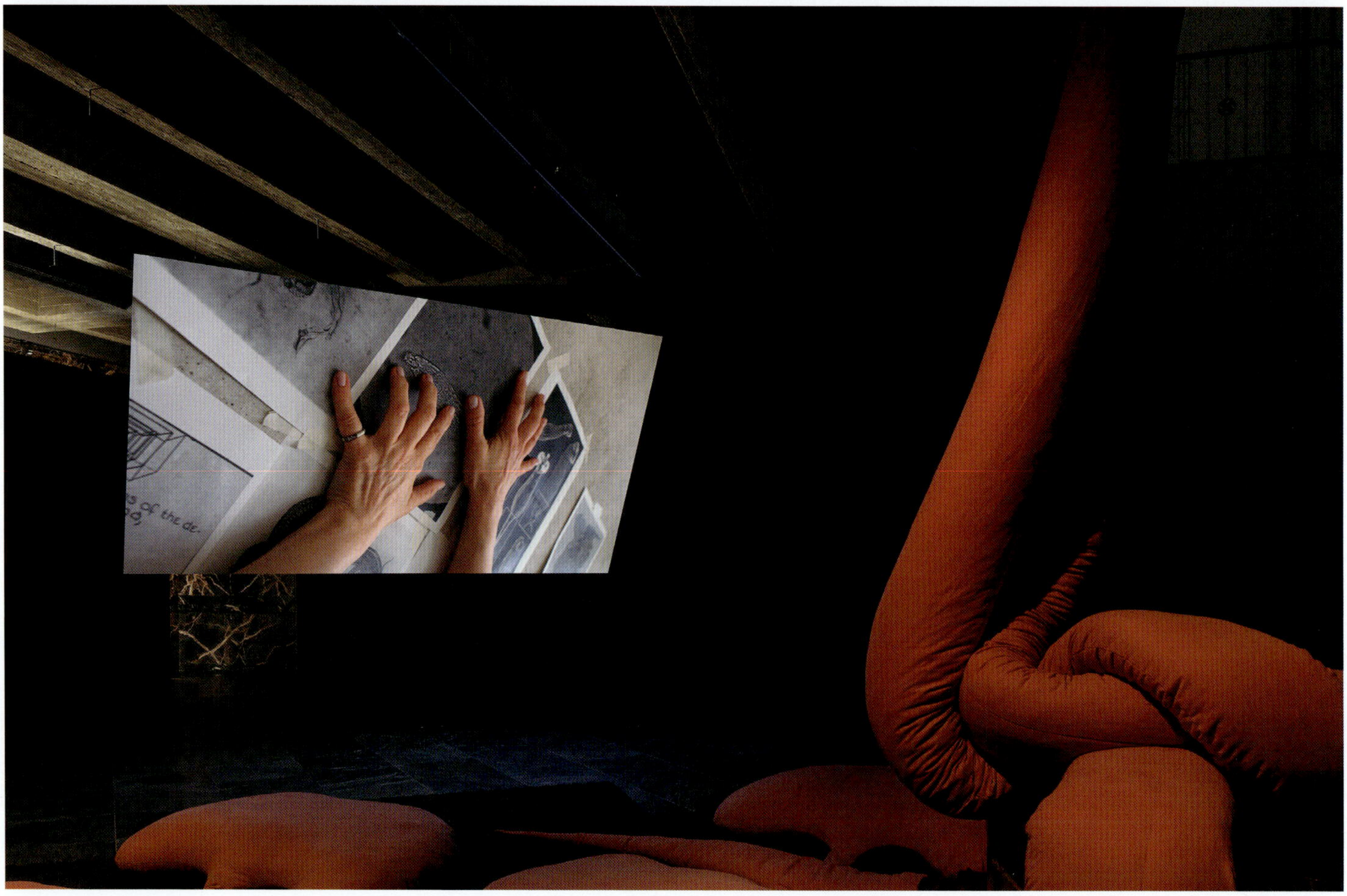

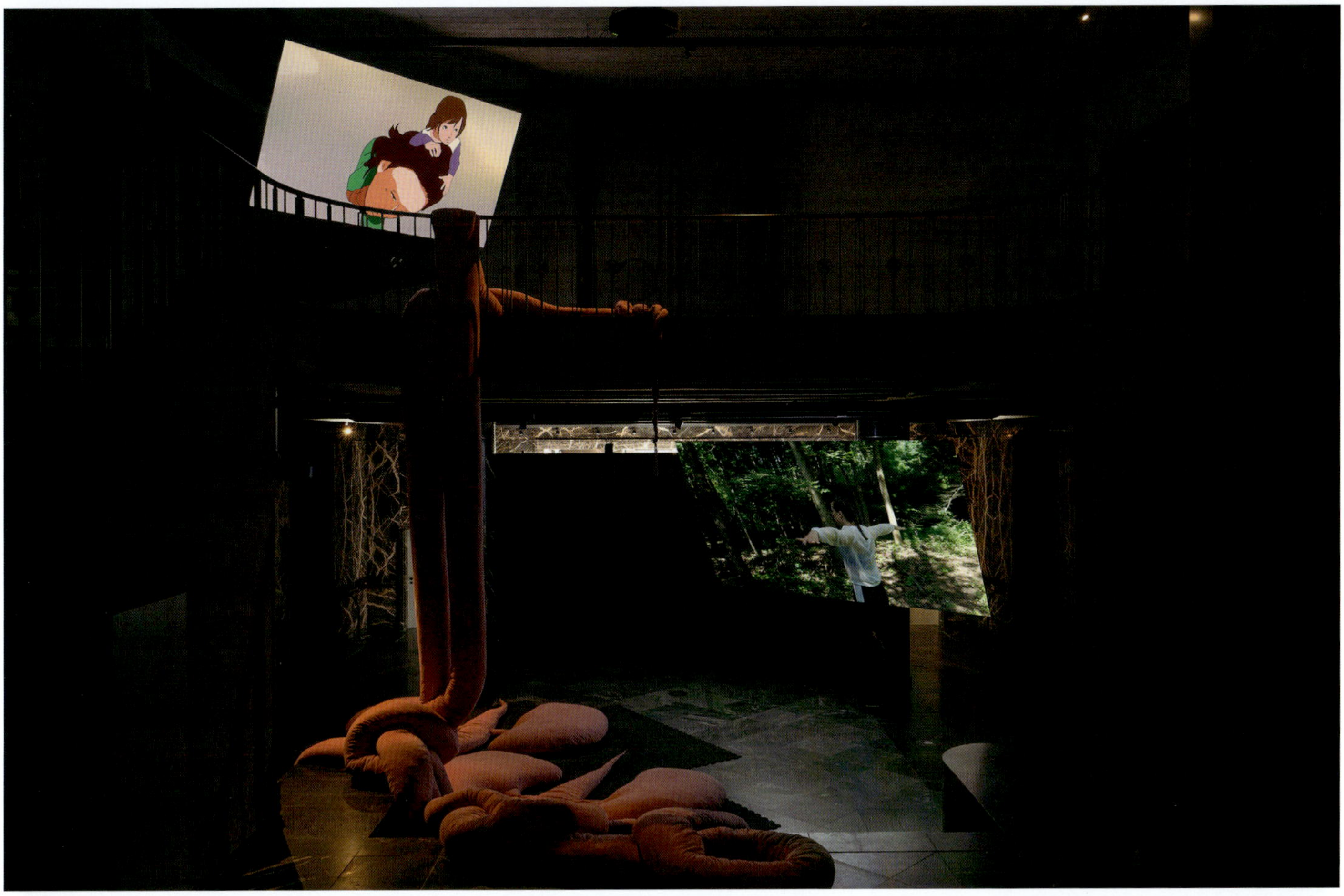

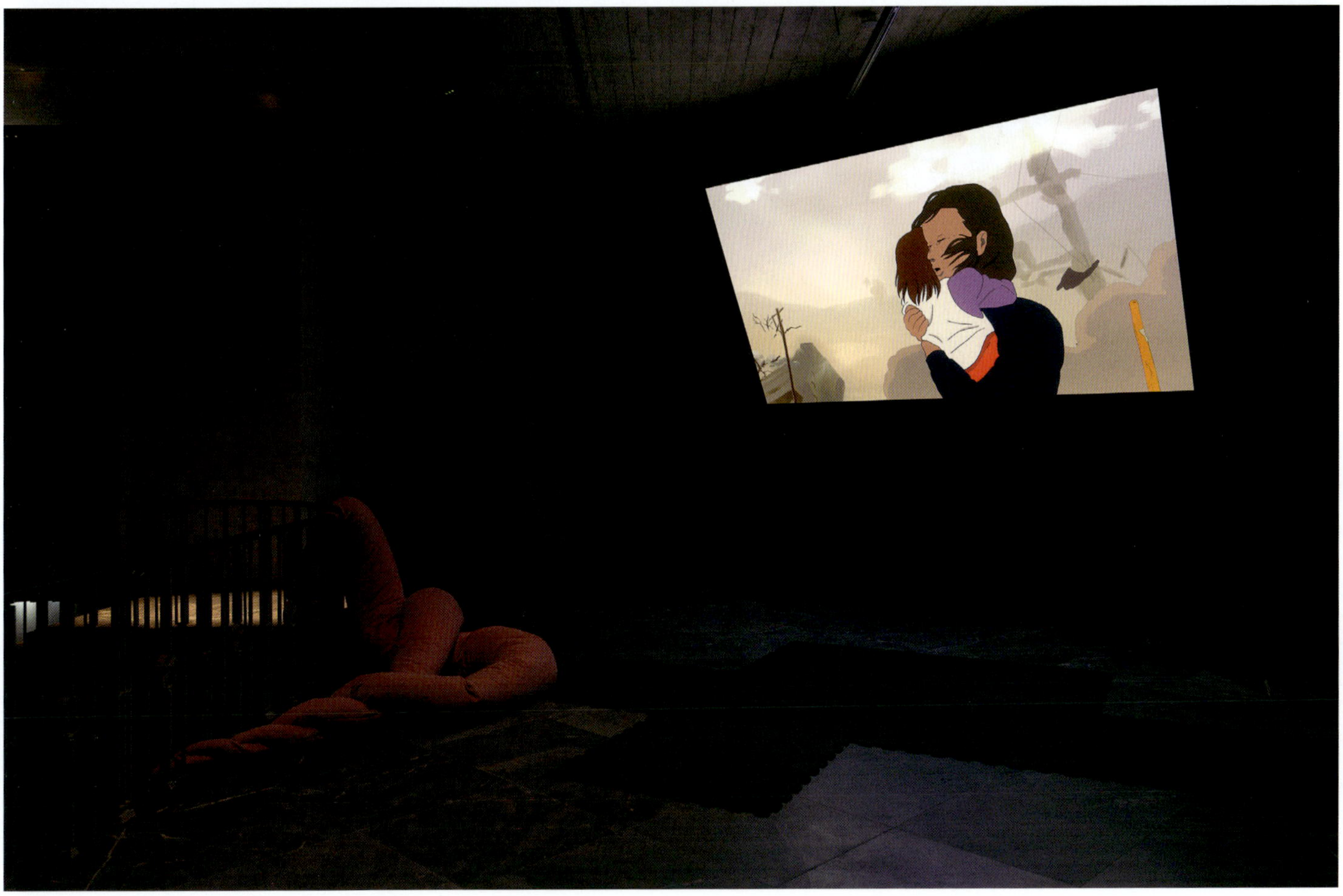

Installation views of the solo exhibition *UNICA* by Blaise Kirschner, Fluentum, Berlin, 2022.
Part of the program series *In Medias Res: Media, (Still) Moving*, 2021–24.

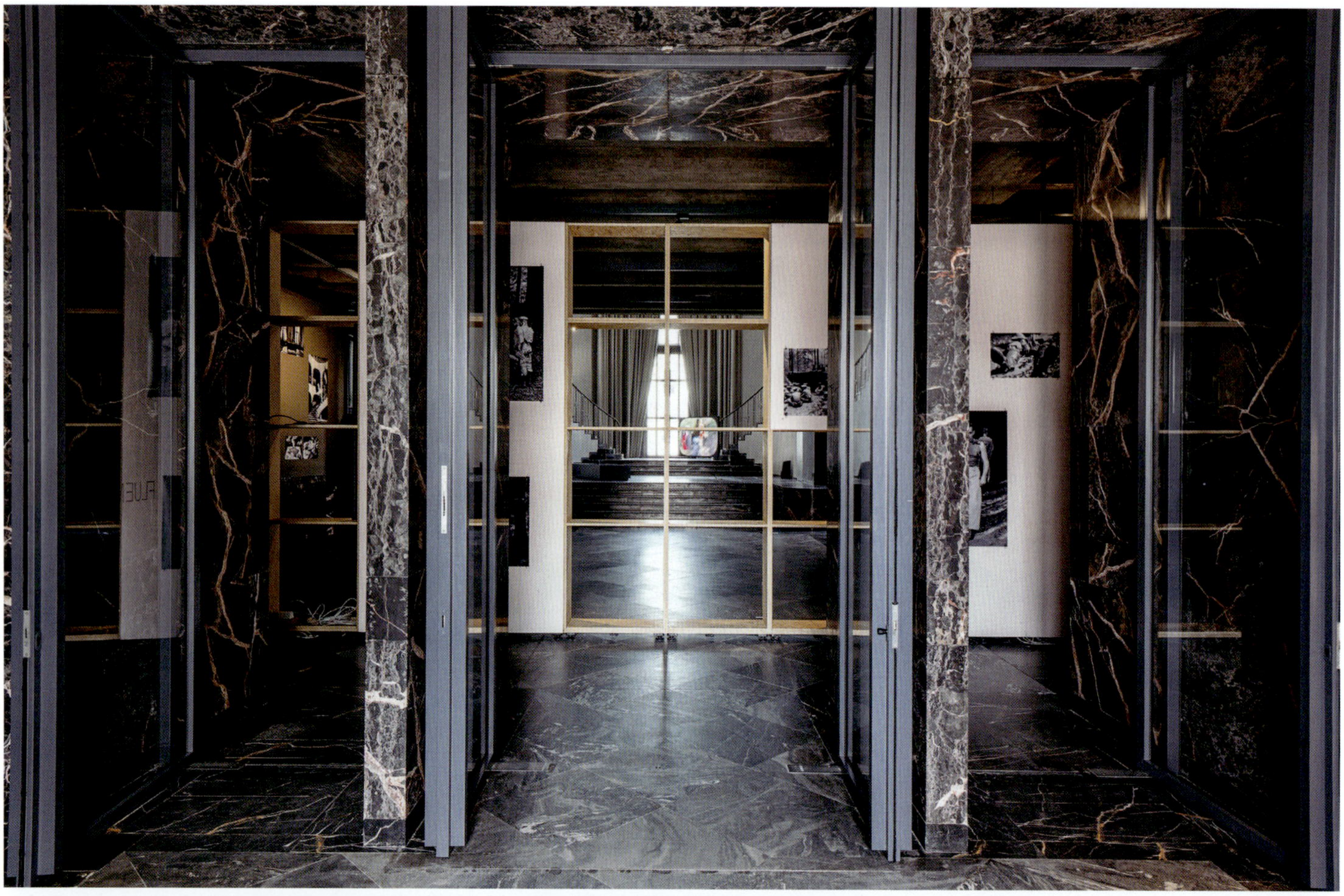

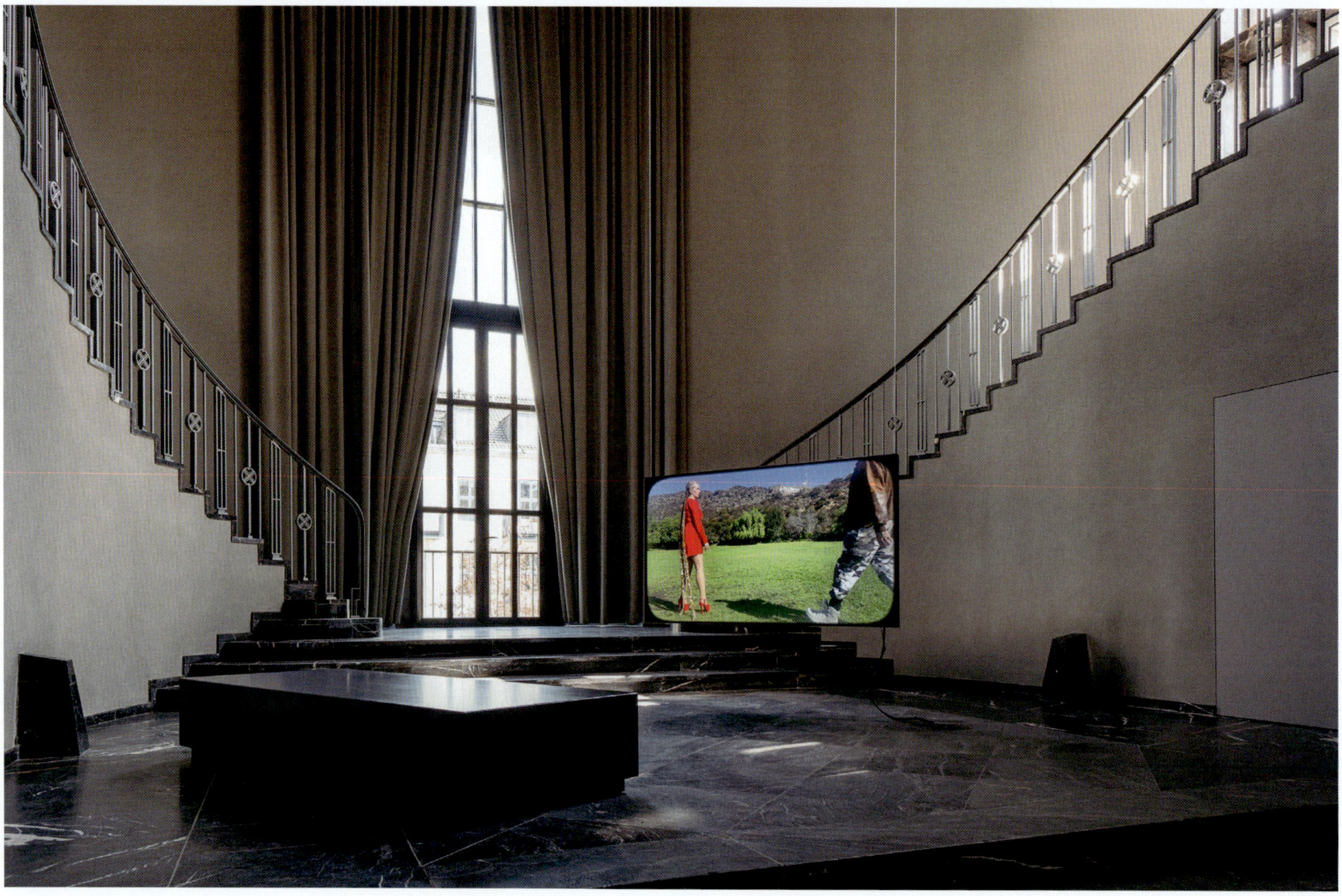

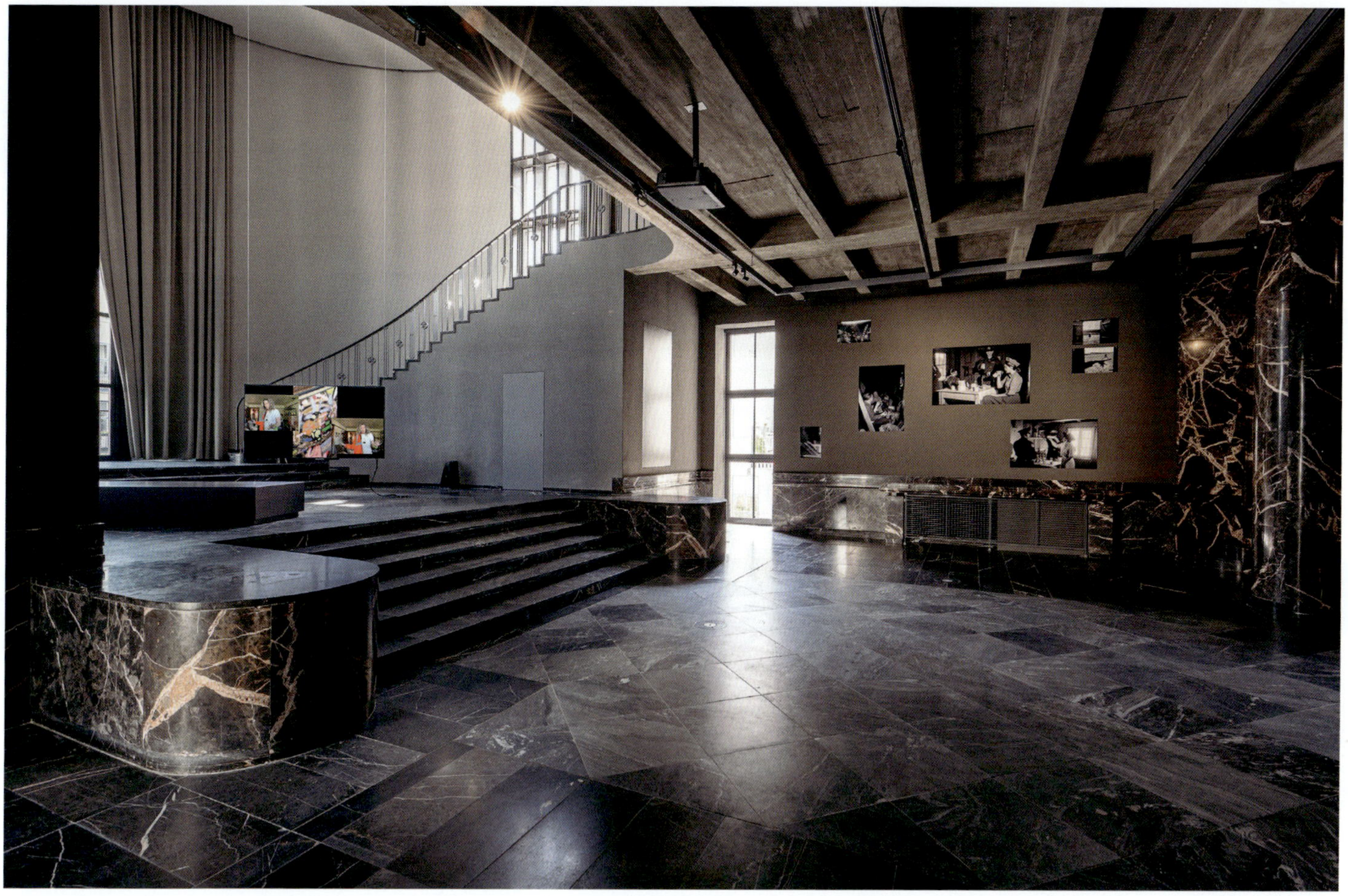

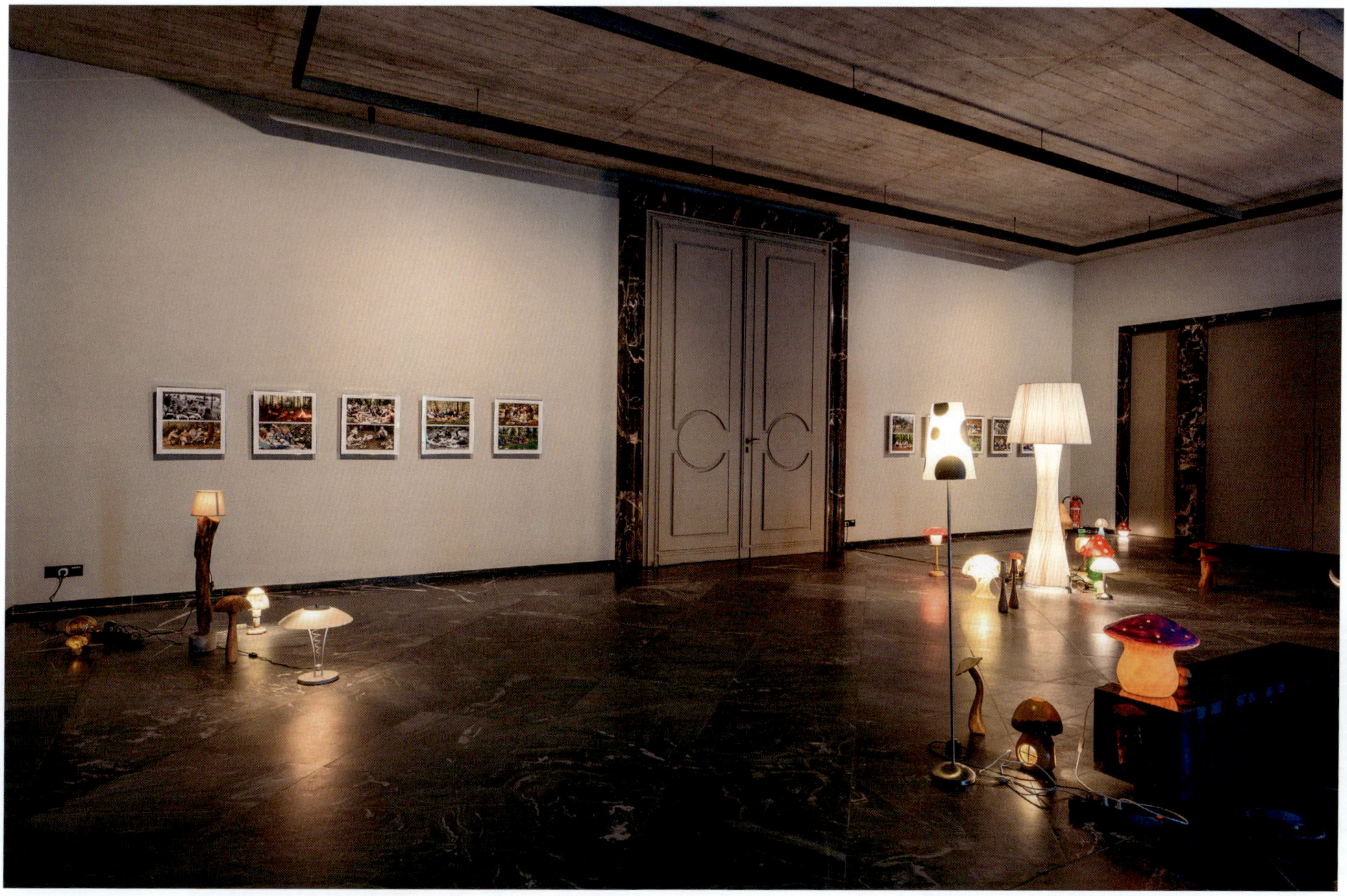

Installation views of the solo exhibition *Trash The Musical* by Loretta Fahrenholz, Fluentum, Berlin, 2023.
Part of the program series *In Medias Res: Media, (Still) Moving*, 2021–24.

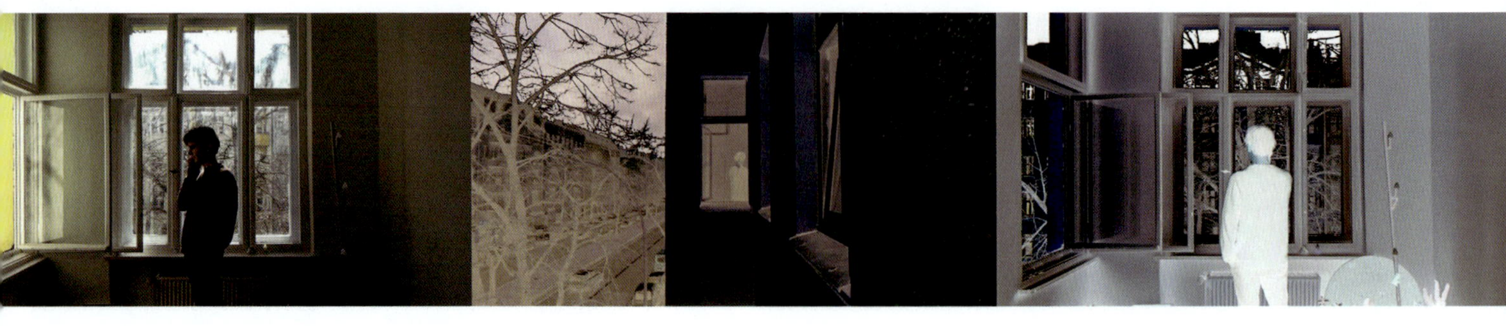

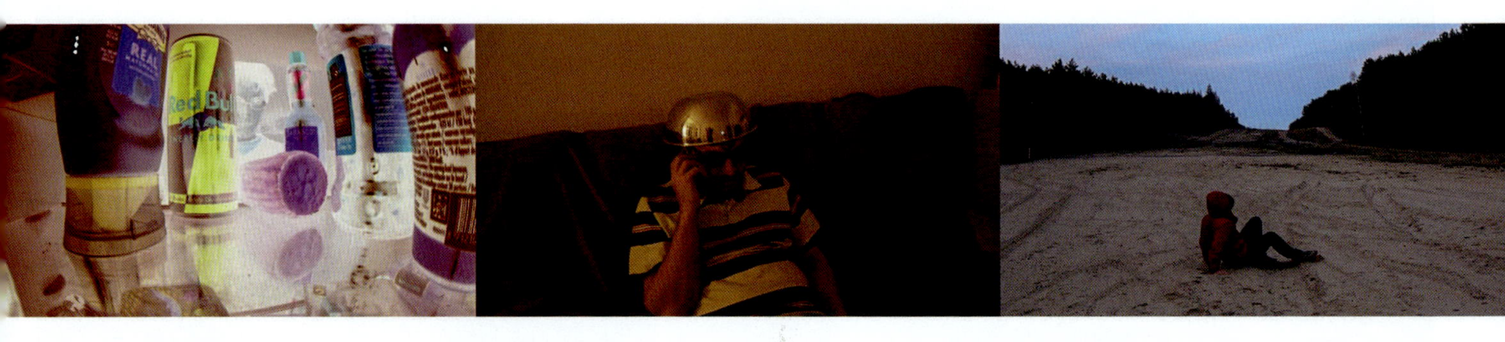

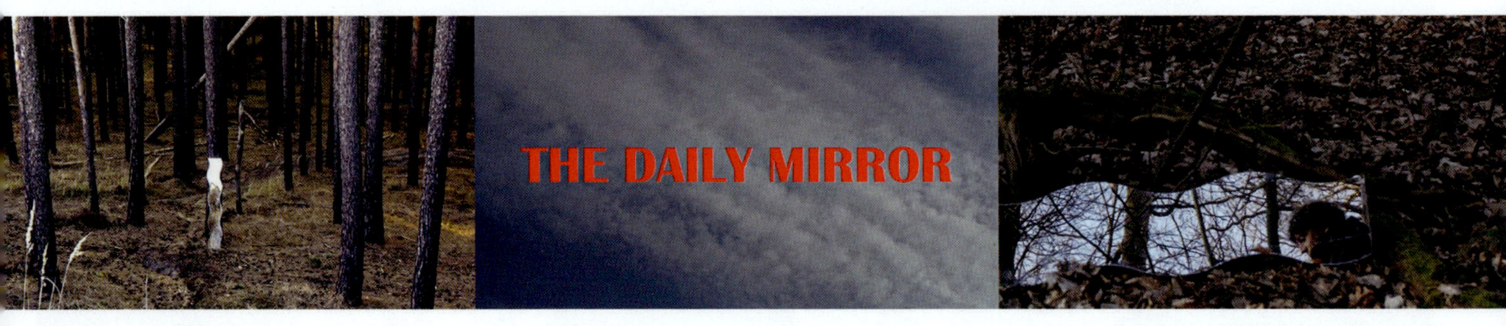
THE DAILY MIRROR

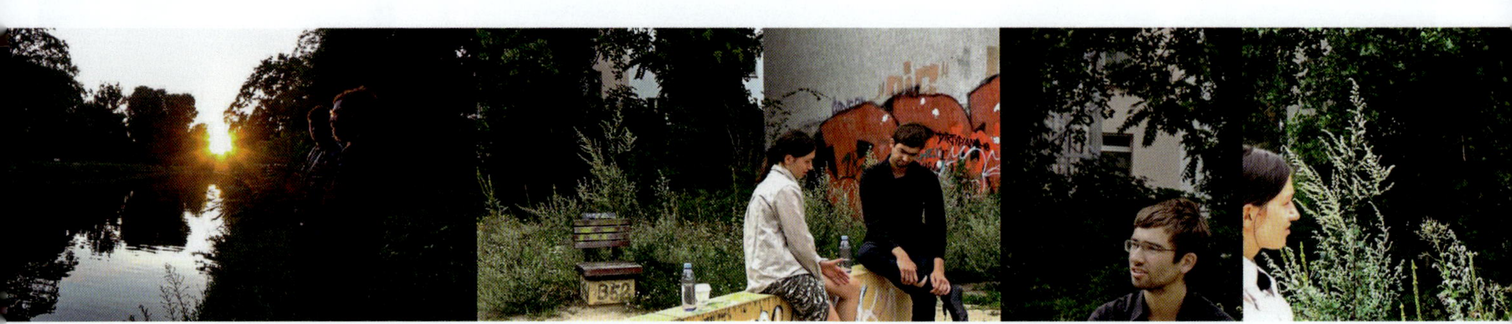

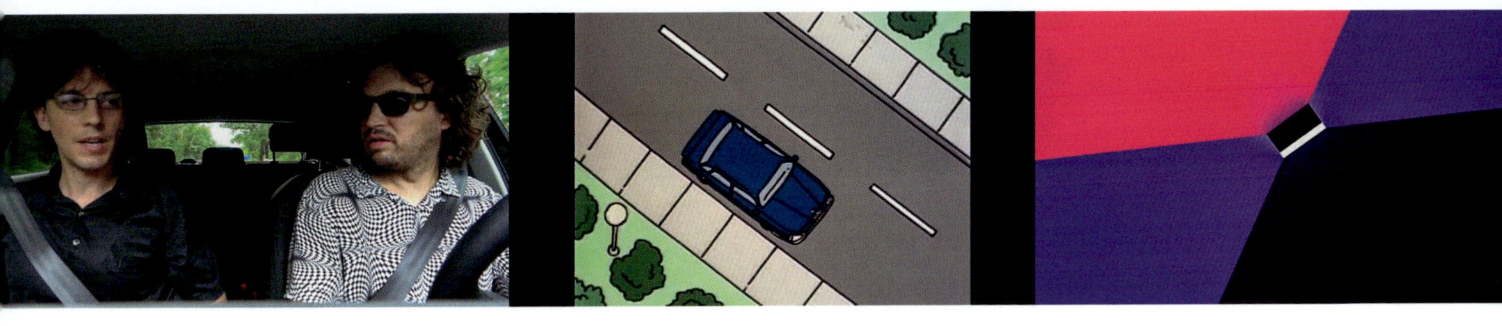

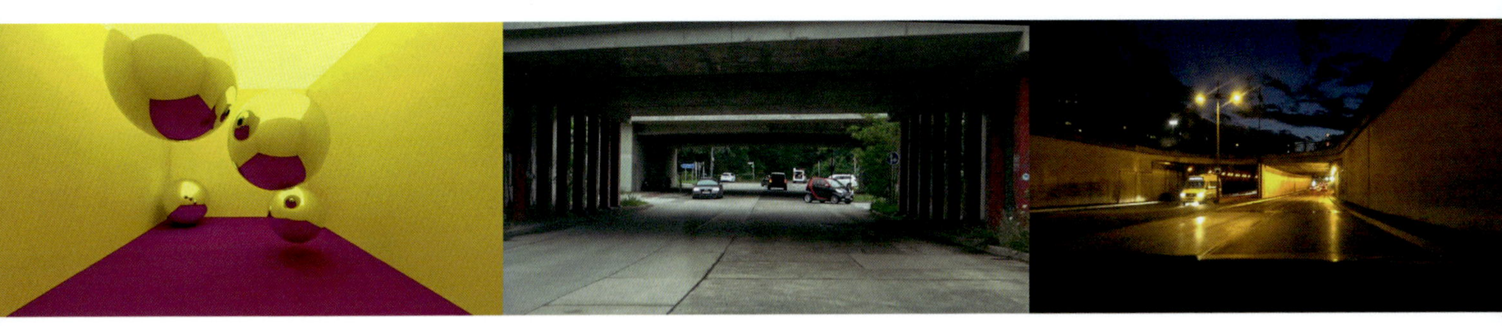

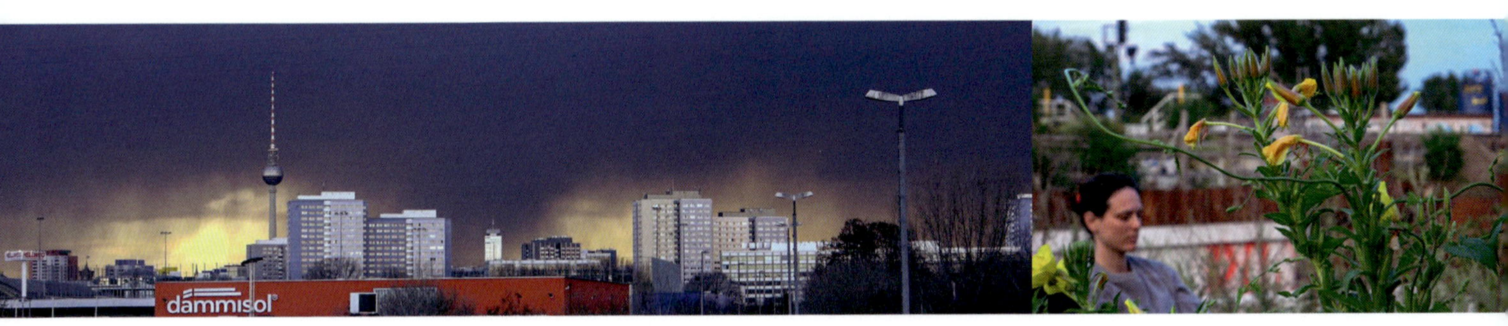

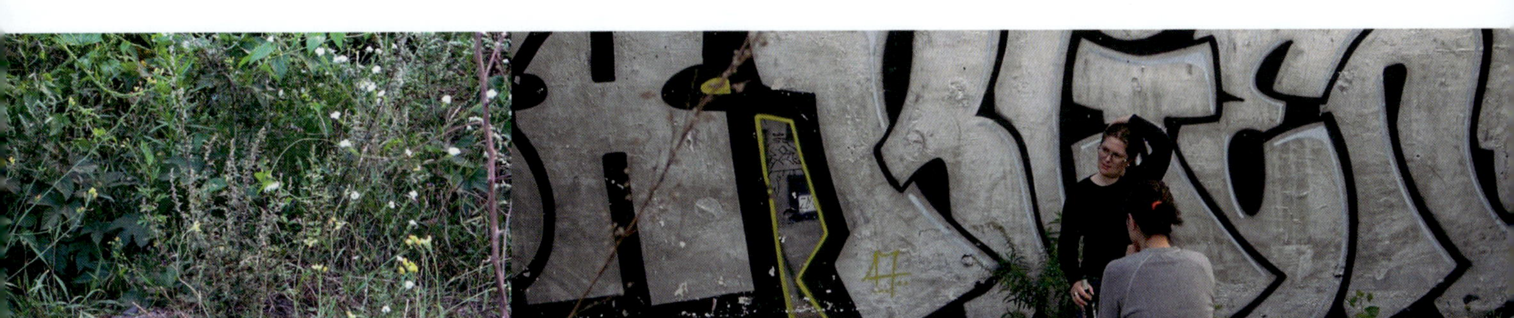

Richard Sides, *Daily Mirrors*, 2024. Collaged video stills from *The Daily Mirror* (2021) in chronological order. Included in the exhibition *Time Without End*, Fluentum, Berlin, 2021.

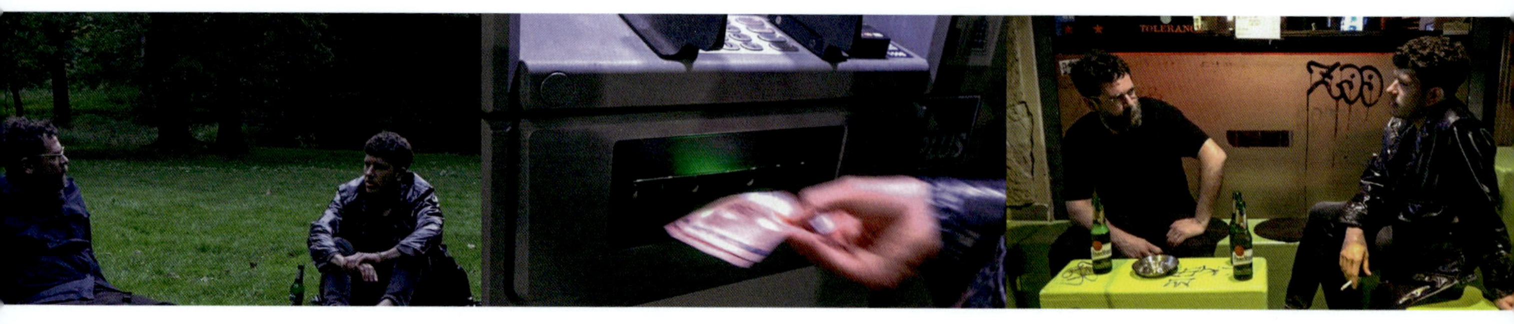

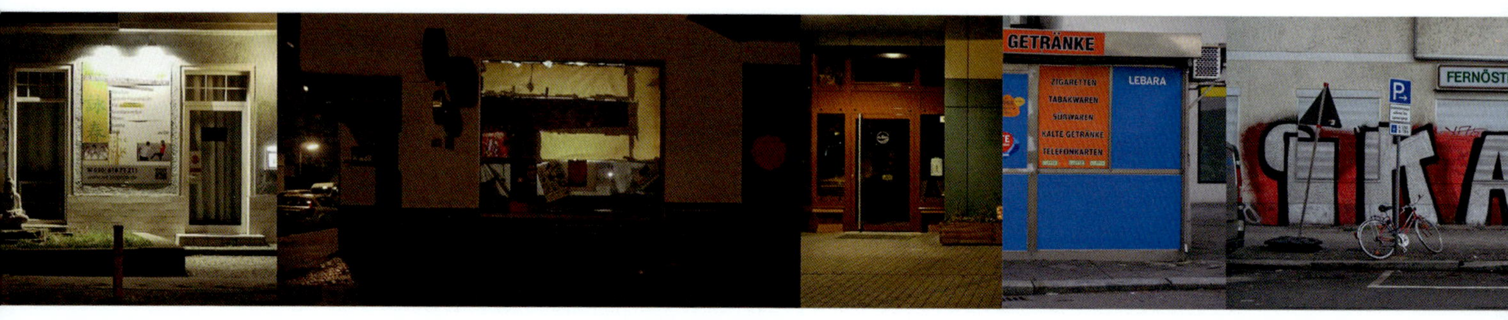

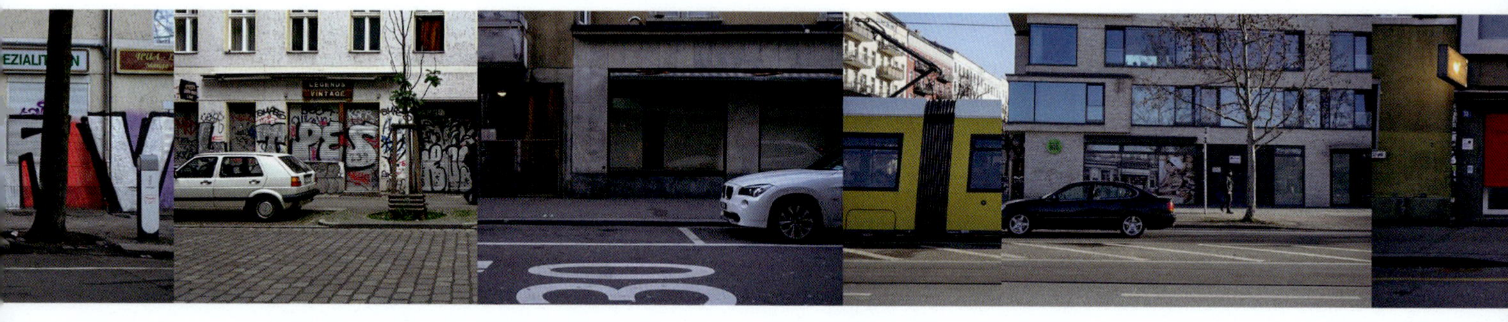

Dennis Brzek and Junia Thiede
In Medias Res—Marble Etchings

As you enter the building that today houses Fluentum's exhibitions, its massive black marble walls and floor subsume you within a spectacle of oppression and veneration. Traversed by brown-and-sand-colored veins, a second web of delicate white carvings can be perceived up close: "Mike Walker 369 Days" or "300 Days" mark a conclusion; "Flatbush," "Chicago," "New York" refer to the origin of their authors; and with "Keep on the Grass," words of wisdom are offered in farewell. This graffiti, which covers the domineering stone like a veil, is the work of US Army soldiers who were stationed here from 1945 onwards. They transformed the walls near the door into a guest book, in which scratching one's own name became a highly personal commentary on the overwrought dramaturgy of the defunct Nazi regime. History itself provides the most fitting image for the palimpsest-like aura of this site. These etchings not only make the past manifest and literally legible, they also expose the material's surreptitious softness, into which traces of time are inscribed; if it were actual marble, as the Nazi architecture pretends—and not just polished sandstone—it would be too solid to write this intricate graffiti.

The publication series *In Medias Res* aims to capture the history and materiality of the building for a contemporary audience, to gather information scattered across various archives, and, last but not least, to serve as a reference source for artists who have been invited by Fluentum to produce new works. As the title *In Medias Res #3: Postproductions* suggests, this final issue focuses on the period since the 1990s, after the fall of the Berlin Wall supposedly buried the conflicts of the twentieth century, which so defined the building, and ushered in a time of cultural and economic prosperity in reunified Berlin. Florian Wüst opens this issue with an extensive essay on the historic failure of a planned Film House at Potsdamer Platz, whose fate will be remembered as a warning sign for the strategic disfigurement of the new capital. At the same time, the then-vacant complex on Clayallee similarly became repurposed for cinema, as it temporarily served as a film set for local and international productions. For period films, it provided the perfect look of an authentic Third Reich location, while films of other genres exploited the forgotten building's cheap rental rates. Fluentum, which is dedicated to showing, producing, and collecting moving-image works, unintentionally continues this history of filmic activation. This issue's structure accordingly follows a loose chronology of films that were shot here, taking them as a starting point to reflect on their staging of history.

With Martin Walz's gory comedy *Killer Condom* (*Kondom des Grauens*; 1996), the "Stars and Stripes" and other paraphernalia returned to the abandoned halls. Unaware of the US military celebrations that once took place here, the film once again turned the building into a stage for German-American subject matter. Based on the eponymous story by gay comics artist Ralf König, the film, which remains little known in Germany, follows bloodthirsty condoms wreaking havoc in New York. In her essay, Elisa R. Linn contextualizes the discursive trails lurking within *Killer Condom* against the historical backdrop of the AIDS crisis, descending into the depths of the reactionary climate that determined the time's social and political discussions.

Dennis Brzek und Junia Thiede
In Medias Res – Ritzungen im Marmor

Beim Betreten des Gebäudes, in dem Fluentum heute Ausstellungen zeigt, beginnt das inszenatorische Spektakel aus Bedrängtheit und Begeisterung der wuchtigen, schwarzen Marmorverkleidung. Durchzogen von braunen und sandfarbenen Adern, offenbart sich aus der Nähe ein zweites Netz aus zarten weißen Ritzungen: „Mike Walker 369 Days" oder „300 Days" ziehen ein Fazit; „Flatbush", „Chicago", „New York" verweisen auf die Herkunft ihrer Autoren; mit „Keep on the Grass" gibt es gleich noch weise Worte zum Abschied. Diese Graffiti, die sich wie ein Schleier über den machteinflößenden Stein legen, stammen von Soldaten der US Army, die hier ab 1945 stationiert waren. Die Wände nahe der Tür wurden von ihnen zum Gästebuch umgemünzt, in dem das Ritzen des eigenen Namens der ganz persönliche Kommentar auf die peinlich-großmächtige Inszenierung des untergegangenen NS-Regimes wird. Das treffendste Bild für die palimpsestartige Präsenz des Ortes bietet die Geschichte gleich selbst. Anhand der Ritzungen wird nicht nur die Vergangenheit manifest und wortwörtlich lesbar, sie erzählt auch von der Nachgiebigkeit des Materials, in das sich Spuren der Zeit einfressen und das, wäre es tatsächlicher Marmor, wie die architektonische NS-Inszenierung vorgaukelt – und nicht allein aufpolierter Sandstein –, zu hart wäre, um so leicht all diese feinen Graffiti aufzunehmen.

Die Publikationsreihe *In Medias Res* hat es sich zur Aufgabe gemacht, die Geschichte und Materialität des Gebäudes für ein zeitgenössisches Publikum einzufangen, die auf verschiedene Archive zerstreuten Informationen zu bündeln und nicht zuletzt auch ein Nachschlagewerk für Künstlerinnen und Künstler bereitzustellen, die von Fluentum eingeladen wurden, neue Werke zu produzieren. Wie im Titel *In Medias Res #3: Postproductions* angelegt, konzentriert sich diese letzte Ausgabe auf die Phase seit den 1990er Jahren, nachdem der Fall der Mauer die das Gebäude so bestimmenden Konflikte des 20. Jahrhunderts vermeintlich begrub und im wiedervereinigten Berlin eine Zeit der kulturwirtschaftlichen Euphorie anbrach. So fühlt Florian Wüst als Auftakt dieser Ausgabe in einem umfangreichen Essay dem historischen Scheitern eines geplanten Filmhauses am Potsdamer Platz nach, dessen Schicksal als ein Menetekel für die strategische Verhunzung der neuen Hauptstadt in Erinnerung bleiben wird. Auch der damals leerstehende Gebäudekomplex an der Clayallee fand vorübergehend eine neue Bestimmung als Filmset für lokale und internationale Produktionen. Für Historienstreifen lieferte er den perfekten Anschein des authentischen Täter-Schauplatzes, für wieder andere Filmteams bedeutete der Leerstand des vergessenen Hauses billige Konditionen. Fluentum, das sich dem Zeigen, Produzieren und Sammeln von Bewegtbild verschreibt, bildet unbeabsichtigt den Anschluss an diese Geschichte filmischer Aktivierung. Die Struktur dieser Ausgabe folgt daher lose einer Chronologie der Filme, die hier gedreht wurden, und nimmt sie zum Ausgangspunkt, um über ihre Inszenierung von Geschichte zu reflektieren.

Mit Hilfe von Martin Walz' Horrorkomödie *Kondom des Grauens* (1996) zogen die „Stars and Stripes" mitsamt anderer Paraphernalia erneut ins verlassene Gebäude ein. Unbehelligt gegenüber den tatsächlich hier stattgefundenen Feier-

When *Valkyrie* was released in 2008, actor Tom Cruise was at the prime of his career—an indestructible action hero capable of defeating all the world's evils. The artist Peter Wächtler was an anonymous extra on the film, which marks the heyday of international production in Potsdam's Babelsberg district, having since subsided. Like a waking dream, his descriptions of the shoot with the eternally indefatigable Cruise revolve around the macho symbolism of cool, something that Richard Hawkins also inspects with a lustful gaze in his Polaroid collage.

The year 2009 saw the acceleration of the transition from analog cinema and its narrative styles to digital surfaces. One proselytizer for traditional processes is Quentin Tarantino, whose blockbuster *Inglourious Basterds* (2009) deployed cinematic fiction to avenge the catastrophe of the Holocaust. Evelyn Kreutzer's essay engages with the ambivalent reception of Tarantino's alternate history and connects the film's self-reflexive elements with current transatlantic debates on the politics of memory. Loretta Fahrenholz's image series *Once Upon a Time in Enemy-Occupied France*, generated by AI, speaks to the instability of images and narratives in today's hypermediated reality, which not only alters our perception of the now, but also how we understand a then.

The 2013 feature film *George* reunites theater and television legend Götz George with his father Heinrich, who died in Soviet captivity. The actor, celebrated since the Weimar era, became one of the Nazi regime's most prominent cultural figures due to his many leading roles in propaganda films. As Thomas Helbig argues in his essay, *George* merges the classic costume drama with docutainment, culminating with the son's psychologically charged self-examination as he reenacts his father's fate. In her artistic contribution *George Overlay*, Maya Schweizer explores the film's reliance on superimposition through long exposures of the scenes set in the interiors that today host Fluentum.

Entering into this seamless amalgam of historical drama and trash comedy genres are the artworks and exhibitions that have been realized and newly produced as part of the *In Medias Res: Media, (Still) Moving* program series. Placed in this catalog side by side, they crack open a film history that extends from the 1990s to the present, emphasizing how the moving image uses time as its material. Like this series of publications, they bear witness to the fact that history always progresses through a detour: from the now into the past—and only then into the future.

Dennis Brzek is Curator at Fluentum. Junia Thiede is Fluentum's Artistic Director. Together, they are the curators of the project series *In Medias Res: Media, (Still) Moving*, 2021–24.

lichkeiten des US-Militärs wurde das Haus wieder zu einer Bühne deutsch-amerikanischen Stoffs. Basierend auf der gleichnamigen Geschichte des schwulen Comiczeichners Ralf König handelt der in Deutschland noch immer wenig bekannte Film von blutrünstigen Kondomen, die in New York ihr Unwesen treiben. In ihrem Essay kontextualisiert Elisa R. Linn die im *Kondom des Grauens* angelegten diskursiven Fährten vor dem zeithistorischen Hintergrund der Aidskrise und steigt dabei in die Untiefen des reaktionären Klimas hinab, das die damaligen gesellschaftspolitischen Debatten bestimmte.

Als *Operation Walküre – Das Stauffenberg-Attentat* im Jahr 2008 in die Kinos kam, stand Schauspieler Tom Cruise auf dem Zenit seiner Karriere als unkaputtbarer Actionheld, der es vermag, alles Übel von der Welt abzuhalten. Für den Film, der zugleich eine inzwischen entrückte Hochzeit des internationalen Produktionstreibens in Potsdam-Babelsberg markiert, war der Künstler Peter Wächtler als anonymer Komparse tätig. Seine an einen Wachtraum erinnernden Beschreibungen vom Dreh mit dem immerwährenden Stehaufmännchen Cruise kreisen um die martialische Symbolik des Cool, die auch Richard Hawkins in seiner Polaroid-Collage mit gierigen Blicken mustert.

Das Jahr 2009 trieb den Kipppunkt von der Welt des analogen Kinos und seinen Erzählweisen in digitale Oberflächen weiter voran. Ein Jünger in traditioneller Sache ist Quentin Tarantino, der mit seinem Blockbuster *Inglourious Basterds* (2009) das Kino nutzte, um die Katastrophe des Holocausts in der Fiktion zu rächen. Evelyn Kreutzers Essay macht die Ambivalenzen in der Rezeption von Tarantinos *Alternate History*-Ansatz produktiv und verbindet die selbstreflexiven Aspekte des Films mit aktuellen, transatlantischen Diskursen zu Erinnerungspolitiken. Loretta Fahrenholz' KI-gestützte Bilderserie *Once Upon a Time in Enemy-Occupied France* spricht von dem medialen Normalzustand der Instabilität von Bildern und ihren Narrativen, die nicht nur unseren Blick auf das Jetzt, sondern auch darauf, wie wir ein Damals verstehen, verändern können.

Im 2013 ausgestrahlten Spielfilm *George* trifft die Theater- und Fernsehlegende Götz George seinen in sowjetischer Gefangenschaft verstorbenen, seit der Weimarer Zeit gefeierten Vater Heinrich, dessen viele Rollen in NS-Propagandafilmen ihn zu einer der präsentesten kulturellen Figuren des Regimes machten. Wie Thomas Helbig in seinem Essay herausstellt, verschmilzt in *George* das Genre des klassischen Kostümdramas mit Dokutainment und kulminiert in einer psychologischen Selbstbefragung des Sohnes, der das väterliche Schicksal gleich selbst nachspielt. In ihrem Bildbeitrag *George Overlay* geht Maya Schweizer diesen Neigungen zur Überlagerung nach, indem sie Langzeitbelichtungen der Szenen anfertigte, die in den Räumen von Fluentum spielen.

Eingebettet in diesen fließenden Genre-Mix aus Historiendrama und Trash-Komödie sind hier auch die künstlerischen Werke sowie Ausstellungen, die im Rahmen der Programmreihe *In Medias Res: Media, (Still) Moving* realisiert und neu produziert worden sind, dokumentiert. So beieinander gestellt eröffnen sie eine Filmgeschichte, die aus den 1990er Jahren hinaus bis in die Gegenwart reicht und dabei unterstreicht, wie Bewegtbild Zeit zu seinem Material macht. Wie auch diese Publikationsreihe bezeugen sie, dass Geschichte immer über einen Umweg voranschreitet: aus dem Jetzt in die Vergangenheit – und erst dann in die Zukunft.

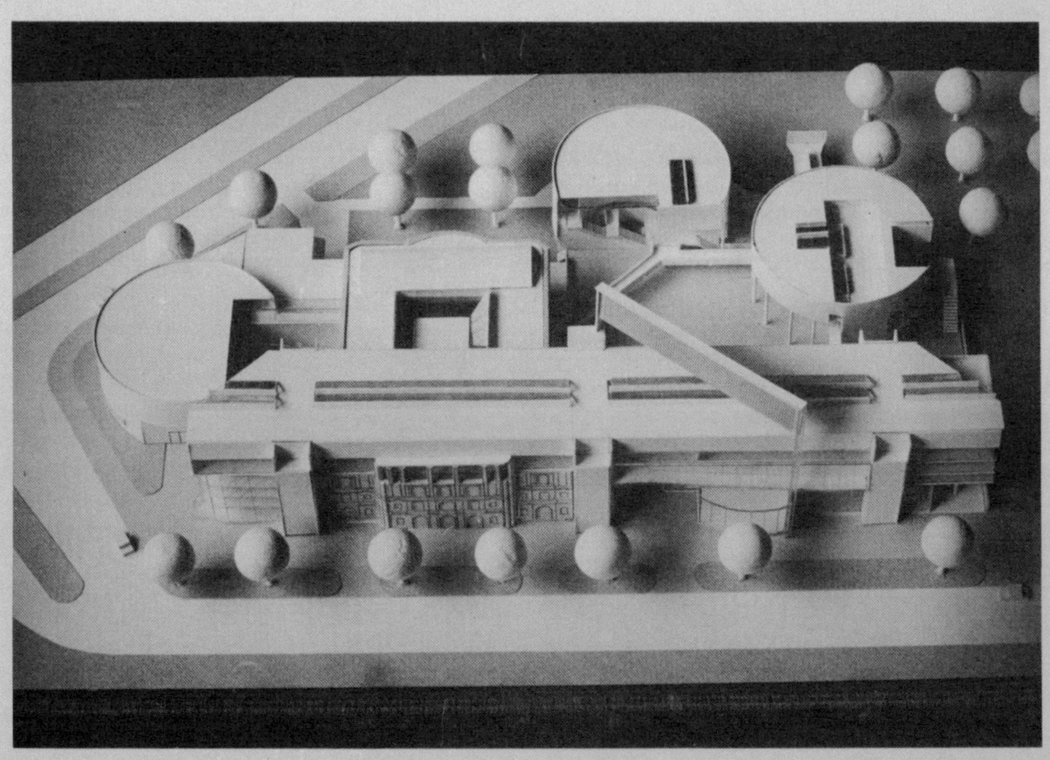

Exhibition poster featuring proposals from the architectural
competition for the Filmhaus Esplanade, May 1985.

Florian Wüst
Beneath the Sands of History—Cinema and Urban Planning Around Potsdamer Platz

"I can't find Potsdamer Platz. Here? This can't be it. Potsdamer Platz is where the Café Josty used to be. In the afternoon I'd go there to chat and have a coffee and watch the crowd." In Wim Wenders's *Wings of Desire* (*Der Himmel über Berlin*; 1987), the bewildered old narrator Homer, played by Curt Bois, walks across a wasteland flanked by the Berlin Wall, on what was once the city's busiest square. Now completely barren, it has become "a flagship for all Berlin anomalies."[1] He is accompanied by Cassiel (Otto Sander), one of the angels who can hear the thoughts of the many lonely people in the ruinous half-city, momentarily infusing them with a feeling of new optimism. Unlike children, adults cannot see the angels nor can they sense their presence. The old man finally collapses into an armchair in the tall grass and vows not to give up until he has found Potsdamer Platz.

Would he find it today? Probably not. The bustling life Homer searches for as he reminisces on his conversations at Café Josty, the former meeting place for Expressionist and New Objectivity artists, can hardly be recognized in the new Potsdamer Platz, with its shopping malls, tourist sights, and high-end hotels—the exception being, perhaps, the annual ten-day Berlinale film festival in February. During that time, at least, the idea of a central, vibrant site for film and cinema in Berlin seems to exist—or rather, seemed. Even Berlinale cannot conceal the fact that film and cinema are disappearing from here. The festival's venues are now dispersed far and wide across the city. The CineStar and IMAX theaters closed at the end of 2019, while the CinemaxX was remodeled and downsized. The Arsenal – Institute for Film and Video Art, the Deutsche Kinemathek – Museum für Film und Fernsehen, and the Deutsche Film- und Fernsehakademie Berlin (DFFB) will soon vacate the former Sony Center.[2] The twenty-five year leases for the "office building with event-driven architecture,"[3] its entrance crowned by the word "Filmhaus" in glowing red letters, is set to expire. Neither the owners nor the three tenants wished to extend the leases.

Filmhaus Esplanade

Wings of Desire cuts to the scene at Potsdamer Platz with Cassiel and the old narrator a second time. The latter muses on the illusion of a world without history, on the hidden "passes, doors, and crevices" that can even be found in flat Berlin. This is where his land of stories would begin: if everyone saw the state of the punctured landscape, "there would be a history without murder or war." The camera pans westward from the Berlin Wall, following flocks of birds past the Staatsbibliothek and the Philharmonie in the distance to the remains of the Hotel Esplanade, which can be made out behind the two protagonists, half-obscured by the elevated maglev train tracks that ran from Gleisdreieck to Kemperplatz between 1984 and 1991, first in testing and then in full passenger service. Constructed in 1908 at Bellevuestraße 16–18a, the grandiose hotel, once the most magnificent and modern building imperial Berlin had to offer, was badly destroyed

Florian Wüst
Unter dem Sand die Geschichte – Kino und Stadtplanung rund um den Potsdamer Platz

„Ich kann den Potsdamer Platz nicht finden. Nein, ich meine hier … Das kann er doch nicht sein! Denn am Potsdamer Platz, da war doch das Café Josty. Nachmittags habe ich mich da unterhalten, dann einen Kaffee getrunken, das Publikum beobachtet." Der alte Erzähler Homer, gespielt von Curt Bois, läuft in Wim Wenders *Der Himmel über Berlin* (1987) unsicher über die von der Mauer flankierte Brache des einst verkehrsreichsten Platzes der Stadt. Nun ein Niemandsland, das „Aushängeschild sämtlicher Berliner Anomalien"[1]. Begleitet wird er von Cassiel (Otto Sander), einem der Engel, die die Gedanken der vielen einsamen Menschen in der ruinösen Halbstadt hören und ihnen für einen Moment neuen Lebensmut einhauchen. Anders als die Kinder können die Erwachsenen die Engel nicht sehen, noch spüren sie ihre Anwesenheit. Schließlich lässt sich der Alte in einen im hohen Gras liegenden Sessel fallen und verspricht, solange nicht aufzugeben, bis er den Potsdamer Platz gefunden hat.

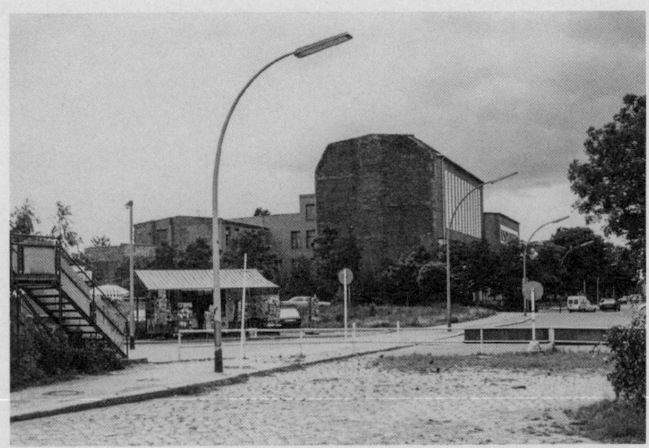

Hotel Esplanade at Potsdamer Platz, June 1984.

Würde er ihn heute finden? Eher nicht. Denn die Lebendigkeit, nach der Homer sucht, wenn er sich seiner Unterhaltungen im Josty erinnert, dem Treff der Künstler*innen des Expressionismus und der Neuen Sachlichkeit, will sich am neuen Potsdamer Platz neben Shopping, Tourismus und Edelhotellerie nicht einstellen. Mit Ausnahme der jährlich zehn Februartage Berlinale vielleicht. Dann scheint oder besser schien die Idee eines zentralen, pulsierenden Berliner Ortes für Film- und Kinokultur aufzugehen. Selbst die Berlinale kann nicht darüber hinwegtäuschen, dass Film und Kino hier im Verschwinden begriffen sind. Die Spielorte des Festivals verteilen sich inzwischen weit über die Stadt. CineStar und IMAX machten Ende 2019 dicht, das CinemaxX wurde umgebaut und verkleinert. Das Arsenal – Institut für Film und Videokunst, die Stiftung Deutsche Kinemathek mit dem Museum für Film und Fernsehen sowie die Deutsche Film- und Fernsehakademie (DFFB) werden das ehemalige Sony Center[2] hinter sich lassen. Die Mietverträge für das „Bürohaus mit Event-Architektur"[3], über dessen Eingang in roten Leuchtbuchstaben „Filmhaus" steht, laufen nach 25 Jahren aus. Weder die Eigentümer noch die drei Mietparteien wollten verlängern.

during World War II. However, the foyer and some halls miraculously survived and could be provisionally repaired. The first balls, fashion shows, and beauty pageants of wrecked postwar Berlin took place here. The erection of the Berlin Wall swiftly relegated the Esplanade to the city's periphery, and it persisted as only a modest hotel and event hall. Despite the dilapidated building's permanent closure in 1981, it continued to be used as a film set. Margarethe von Trotta filmed *Marianne and Juliane* (*Die bleierne Zeit*; 1981) here, and Nick Cave and the Bad Seeds performed at the Esplanade in *Wings of Desire*. Cassiel's partner Damiel (Bruno Ganz) and the trapeze artist Marion (Solveig Dommartin) meet at the bar during the concert. She had previously seen him in a dream. Damiel's encounter with her instigates his descent into earthly life, where he becomes a human among humans.

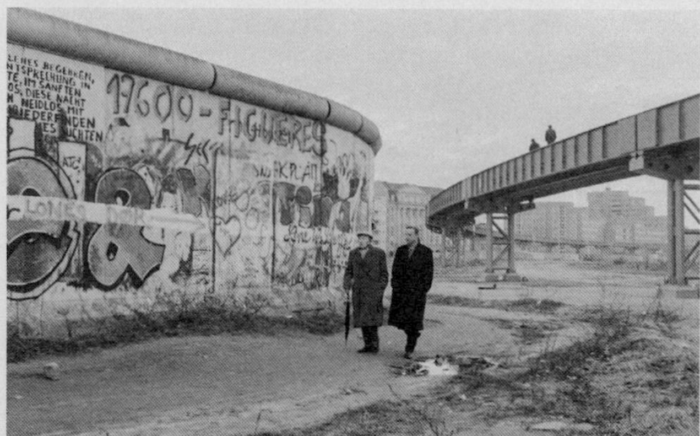

Der Himmel über Berlin (*Wings of Desire*), Wim Wenders, 1987 (film still).

The location's postwar cultural history inspired the Senate to hold an architectural competition in the mid-1980s for a Filmhaus (Film House) around the hotel's remains. The Freunde der deutschen Kinemathek, together with the Arsenal cinema,[4] the Deutsche Kinemathek, and the DFFB were to be given a shared center, complemented by a film museum, a film library, rooms for rent available to the film industry, and a restaurant and cafeteria.[5] In spring 1985, the jury opted for the futuristic design by Amsterdam architect Herman Hertzberger. It envisioned a segmented building complex that integrated the old Esplanade with a bridge-like superstructure, in the back of which barrel-shaped constructions connected by footbridges would be arranged like film cans: a film city within the city. The state and federal governments—the property belonged to the federally owned Industrieverwaltungsgesellschaft mbH—subsequently argued over who would be responsible for its construction and funding; political disruptions further delayed its realization.[6] It was not until October 27, 1990, three weeks into reunification, that the *taz* newspaper proclaimed, "Esplanade Filmhaus at Potsdamer Platz to be built."[7] But nothing happened. In summer 1991 the property was sold to Sony for a laughable price.

Filmhaus Esplanade

Der Himmel über Berlin schneidet ein zweites Mal auf die Szene mit Cassiel und dem alten Erzähler am Potsdamer Platz. Letzterer sinniert über die Illusion einer geschichtslosen Welt, über die verborgenen „Pässe, Pforten und Durchschlüpfe", die auch das flache Berlin habe. Dort fange sein Land der Erzählung an: Würden alle diese Perforiertheit der Landschaft sehen, „gäbe es eine Geschichte ohne Totschlag und Krieg". Die Kamera schwenkt von der Mauer Richtung Westen, Vogelschwärmen folgend, vorbei an Staatsbibliothek und Philharmonie in der Ferne bis zu den Resten des Hotel Esplanade, die hinter den beiden Protagonisten auszumachen sind, halb verdeckt durch die Hochtrasse der Magnetbahn, die zwischen 1984 und 1991 zuerst im Versuchsbetrieb, dann im Fahrgastbetrieb vom Gleisdreieck zum Kemperplatz führte. Das 1908 in der Bellevuestraße 16–18a erbaute Grandhotel, einst das Prachtvollste und Fortschrittlichste, was das kaiserliche Berlin zu bieten hatte, wurde im Zweiten Weltkrieg stark zerstört. Foyer und einige Säle aber blieben auf wundersame Weise stehen und konnten notdürftig instand gesetzt werden. Hier fanden die ersten Bälle, Modeschauen und Misswahlen des zertrümmerten Berlins statt. Der Mauerbau versetzte das Esplanade mit einem Schlag an den Rand, nur ein bescheidener Hotel- und Veranstaltungsbetrieb ließ sich aufrechterhalten.

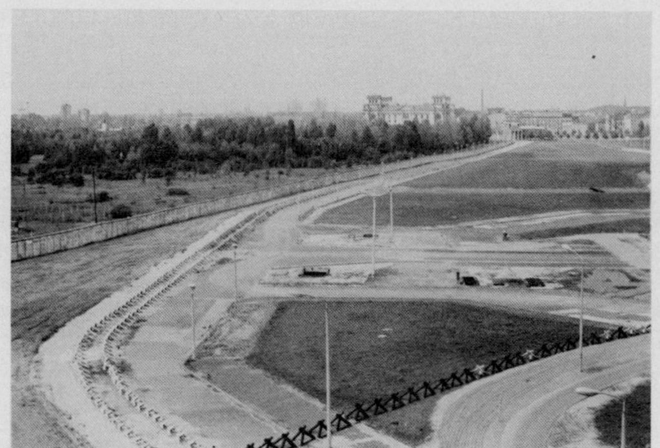

View of the Wall from Haus Vaterland, ca. 1976.

Trotz der Sperrung des maroden Gebäudes im Jahr 1981 wurde es weiter als Filmkulisse genutzt. Margarethe von Trotta drehte für *Die bleierne Zeit* (1981), in *Der Himmel über Berlin* spielt der Auftritt von Nick Cave and the Bad Seeds im Esplanade. Cassiels Kompagnon Damiel (Bruno Ganz) und die Trapezkünstlerin Marion (Solveig Dommartin) treffen sich während des Konzerts an der Bar. Sie sah ihn im Traum. Er fand in der Begegnung mit ihr den letzten Anstoß, ins irdische Leben herabzusteigen, Mensch unter Menschen zu werden.

Die kulturelle Nachkriegsgeschichte des Ortes inspirierte den Senat dazu, Mitte der 1980er Jahre einen Architekturwettbewerb zur Errichtung eines Filmhauses rund um den Hotel-Torso auszuschreiben. Die Freunde der deutschen Kinemathek mit dem Kino Arsenal[4], die Stiftung Deutsche Kinemathek und die DFFB sollten ein gemeinsames Zentrum erhalten, ergänzt durch ein Filmmuseum, eine Filmbibliothek,

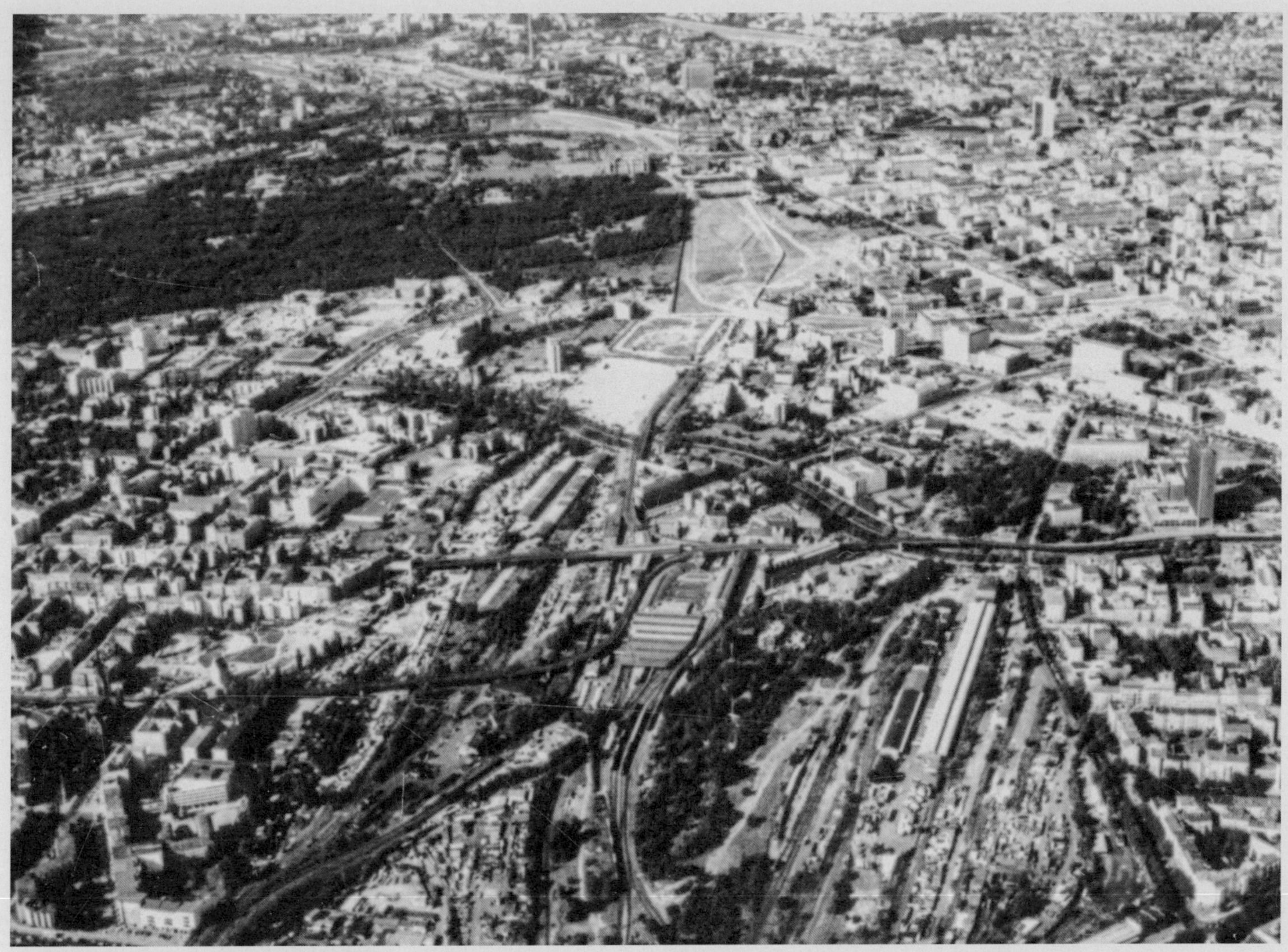

Aerial view of the Central Area, August 1984.

Central Area

At the time, Harun Farocki vehemently polemicized against these plans for a West Berlin center of film art, a sort of "guild house" where he would be forced to meet "the film crowd," as if film were merely a craft, "something as commonplace and necessary as a shoe." In order to strengthen film, he felt that the film crowd should not convene and flatter their egos but rather disperse.[8] Another criticism, of "urban planning and architects" taking over Berlin's geographical center, had already been expressed before the idea of a Filmhaus had even been verbalized. Architectural critic and urban planner Dieter Hoffmann-Axthelm viewed the fact that people were "tearing—the treacherous butcher's language—the 'tenderloin' out of each other's fangs and already populating red, green, and blue colored plans with apartment blocks, factories, expressways, and the like" as an indication that the

Räume zur Anmietung durch die Filmbranche sowie einen Restaurant- und Cafeteriabereich.[5] Das Preisgericht entschied sich im Frühjahr 1985 für den futuristisch anmutenden Entwurf des Amsterdamer Architekten Herman Hertzberger. Dieser sah vor, das alte Esplanade durch einen brückenhaften Überbau in einen gegliederten Gebäuderiegel zu integrieren, in dessen Rücken sich tonnenförmige, über Stege verbundene Baukörper, Filmdosen gleich, anordnen: eine Filmstadt in der Stadt. Land und Bund – Eigentümerin des Grundstücks war die bundeseigene Industrieverwaltungsgesellschaft mbH – stritten in Folge über Bauträgerschaft und Finanzierung, auch politische Störfeuer trugen zur Verzögerung des Baubeginns bei.[6] Erst am 27. Oktober 1990, die Wiedervereinigung war bereits drei Wochen alt, schrieb die taz: „Das Filmhaus Esplanade am Potsdamer Platz kann gebaut werden."[7] Doch es passierte nichts. Im Sommer 1991 wurde das Grundstück für einen läppischen Preis an Sony verkauft.

Florian Wüst

"center" was in danger.[9] The most symbolic meeting point of the divided world—especially true of Potsdamer Platz—had not only gradually turned into an urban desert,[10] it had become a double periphery. "What could be torn down in East and West was torn down, while the focus shifted to seemingly unburdened subcenters. What remained in between was a historical disaster zone that was soon empty," Hoffmann-Axthelm continued in his pointed essay "Berliner Zentrum," published in *Bauwelt* in December 1981.[11] Reconstruction should honor the fact of destruction, not erase it or turn it into a harmless cultural episode.[12] British artist Cynthia Beatt explored the deeper meaning of emptiness in her short film *Fury is a Feeling Too* (*Böse zu sein ist auch ein Beweis von Gefühl*; 1983), which oscillates between anger and understanding, documentary and mise-en-scène: "I see architecture as a language, which is linked to the human soul. Consequently the destruction of the text is also the destruction of the human

Zentraler Bereich

Harun Farocki polemisierte seinerzeit heftig gegen die Pläne einer zentralen Westberliner Repräsentanz der Filmkunst, eines „Innungshäuschens", in dem er „all den Filmmenschen" zu begegnen hätte. Als wäre der Film reines Handwerk, „etwas Alltägliches und Notwendiges wie ein Schuh". Um den Film stark zu machen, müssten sich die Filmmenschen nicht zusammensetzen und aufplustern, sondern auseinandergehen.[8] Eine anders gerichtete Kritik, die Kritik an der Bemächtigung der geografischen Mitte Berlins durch „Stadtplanung und Architekten", lag schon auf dem Tisch, als die Idee eines Filmhauses noch gar nicht laut gedacht war. Dass diese „sich die – verräterische Metzgersprache – ‚Filetstücke' gegenseitig aus den Zähnen reißen und auf rot, grün und blau kolorierten Plänen bereits mit Wohnschachtel, Fabrik, Schnellstraße und dergleichen Vertrautem mehr bestücken," sah der Archi-

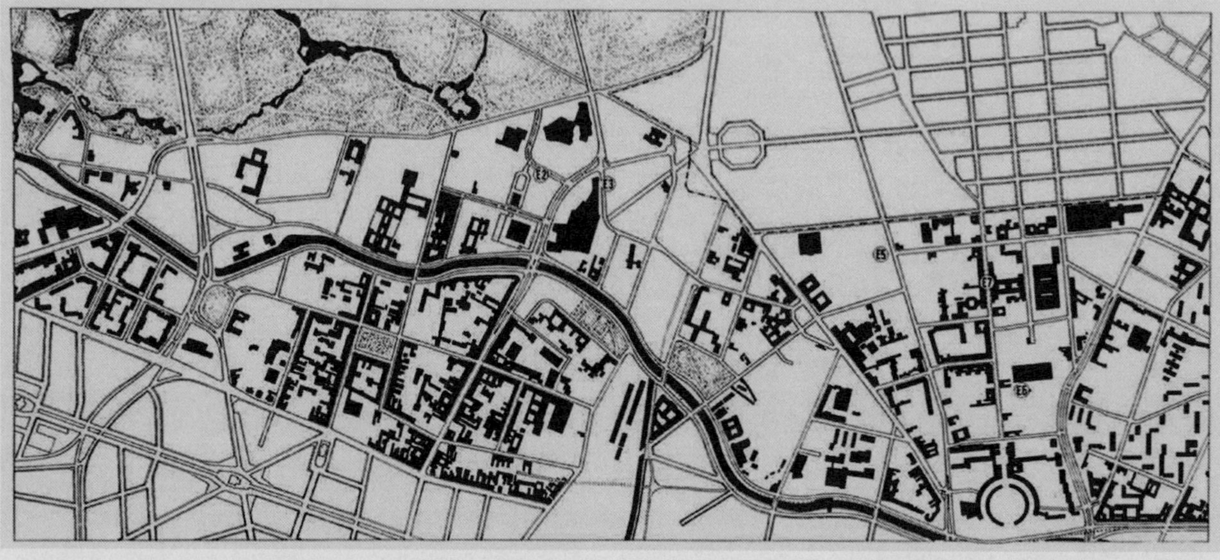

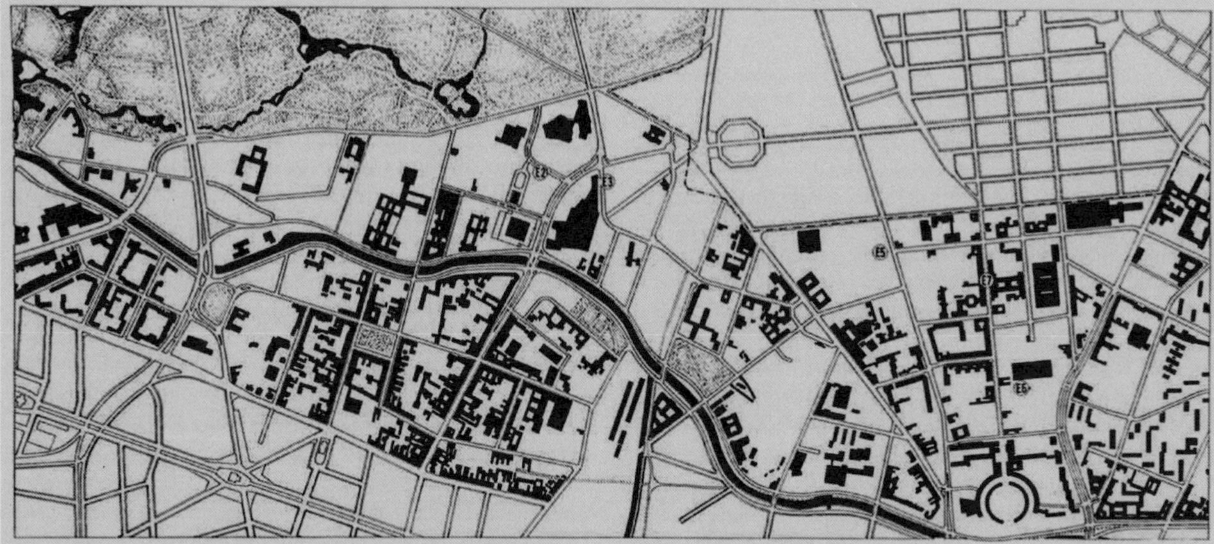

Schematic drawings of the IBA development areas, 1981.
Above: the site's actual state at the time; below: the proposed design.

soul." The camera inches its way over the Philharmonie's dirty golden skin, Martin-Gropius-Bau's patched-up masonry, the ruined fragments of Anhalter Bahnhof. Inspired by the view from her studio window, all of the film's locations are in the vicinity of Potsdamer Platz. In this landscape, whose ground once bore National Socialism's center of power, Beatt recognized that the loss of identity of postwar Germany concealed the cultural violence the country had committed behind arrogance and xenophobia.

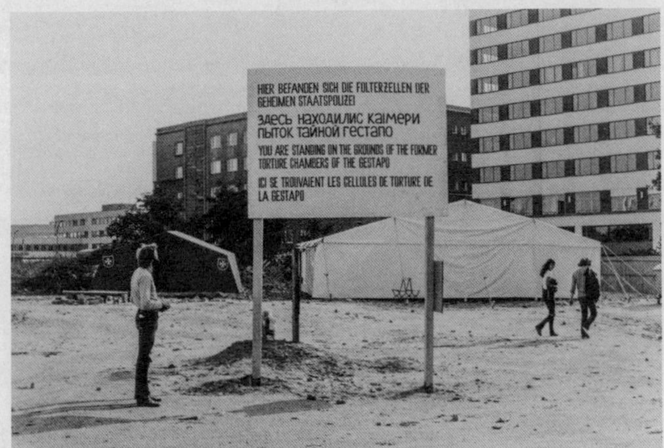

Prinz-Albrecht terrain, which later became the Topography of Terror Documentation Center, ca. 1980.

The euphemism for Berlin's western center was conceived as a Central Area (Zentraler Bereich)—only administrative language can be this innocuously factual. Beginning in Nordhafen, it stretched over Spreebogen, the Reichstag, the eastern part of Tiergarten, the former diplomatic district, Kulturforum, Potsdamer Platz, Anhalter Bahnhof, and Gleisdreieck, before culminating with the Yorckbrücken in the south. That this area came into focus at all in the early 1980s—and was made the subject of an ambitious planning process, albeit one that remained purely theoretical—was due to a fundamental shift away from clear-cut redevelopment (focused on large-scale demolition and new construction) and back to the historic city. Two principles paved the way out of this urban planning crisis: "careful urban renewal" and "critical reconstruction." They formed the basis for the International Building Exhibition (IBA) 1984/87, which facilitated experimentation for "saving the ruined city" under the slogan "The inner city as a place to live."[13] Under the direction of Hardt-Waltherr Hämer, who had organized a program of "urban repair" and citizen participation as the redevelopment commissioner at Klausenerplatz, the IBA-Alt carried out a large number of pilot projects for the preservation, modernization, and conversion of existing buildings in Kreuzberg and Schöneberg. The IBA-Neu, headed by architect Josef Paul Kleihues, launched a housing construction program that combined a consideration for existing structures with a reassessment of the city's historic layout. As early as 1977, Kleihues rehabilitated residential perimeter blocks with Block 270 on Vinetaplatz in the Wedding Brunnenstraße redevelopment area. Such building complexes had been seen by modernism (both pre- and postwar) as epitomizing social misery and the

tekturkritiker und Stadtplaner Dieter Hoffmann-Axthelm als ein Anzeichen dafür, dass die „Mitte" in Gefahr ist.[9] Die symbolträchtigste Nahtstelle der geteilten Welt, allem voran der Potsdamer Platz, hatte sich nicht nur sukzessive zur städtischen Wüste verwandelt[10], sie wurde zur doppelten Peripherie. „Man riß in Ost und West ab, was abreißbar war, und konzentrierte sich auf scheinbar unbelastete Teilzentren. Dazwischen blieb eine historische Katastrophenzone, die bald nur noch leer war," so Hoffmann-Axthelm weiter in seinem pointiert verfassten Essay „Berliner Zentrum" in der *Bauwelt* vom Dezember 1981.[11] Ein Wiederaufbau müsse die Tatsache der Zerstörung festhalten, nicht löschen oder aus ihr eine harmlose Kulturveranstaltung machen.[12] Der tieferen Bedeutung der Leere geht die britische Künstlerin Cynthia Beatt in ihrem zwischen Wut und Verständnis, Dokumentation und Inszenierung changierenden Kurzfilm *Böse zu sein ist auch ein Beweis von Gefühl* (1983) nach: „Ich sehe Architektur als eine Sprache, die mit der Seele der Menschen verbunden ist. Also ist die Zerstörung des Textes auch eine Zerstörung der Menschenseele." Die Kamera tastet über die schmutzig-goldene Haut der Philharmonie, das geflickte Mauerwerk des Martin-Gropius-Baus, das Ruinenfragment des Anhalter Bahnhofs. Inspiriert vom Blick aus ihrem Atelierfenster liegen alle Drehorte des Films im Umfeld des Potsdamer Platzes. In dieser Landschaft, deren Boden einst das Machtzentrum des Nationalsozialismus trug, erkennt Beatt den Identitätsverlust eines Nachkriegsdeutschlands, das den verübten Kulturbruch hinter Arroganz und Fremdenfeindlichkeit versteckt.

So unverfänglich sachlich kann nur Verwaltungssprache sein: Der Planungstopos für die Berliner Mitte-West lautete „Zentraler Bereich". Er reichte vom Nordhafen über Spreebogen, Reichstag, den östlichen Teil des Tiergartens, das ehemalige Diplomatenviertel, Kulturforum, Potsdamer Platz, Anhalter Bahnhof und Gleisdreieck bis zu den Yorckbrücken im Süden. Dass dieses Areal Anfang der 1980er Jahre überhaupt in den Fokus rückte und zum Gegenstand eines ambitionierten, wenn auch im Diskursraum verbliebenen Planungsverfahrens wurde, war einem grundsätzlichen Umdenken geschuldet, fort von der Kahlschlagsanierung durch großflächigen Abriss und Neubau und zurück zur historischen Stadt. Diesen Weg aus der städtebaulichen Krise ebneten zwei unterschiedliche Leitlinien: die „behutsame Stadterneuerung" und die „kritische Rekonstruktion". Sie bildeten die Grundlage der Internationalen Bauausstellung (IBA) 1984/87, die unter dem Motto „Die Innenstadt als Wohnort" ein Experimentierfeld zur „Rettung der kaputten Stadt" aufmachte.[13] Die IBA-Alt unter der Leitung von Hardt-Waltherr Hämer, der als Sanierungsbeauftragter am Klausenerplatz Stadtreparatur und Bürger*innenbeteiligung organisiert hatte, führte eine Vielzahl von Pilotprojekten zur erhaltenden Modernisierung und Umnutzung bestehender Gebäude in Kreuzberg und Schöneberg durch. Die IBA-Neu, der der Architekt Josef Paul Kleihues vorstand, legte ein Wohnungsbauprogramm auf, das das Bewusstsein für das Bestehende mit der Neubewertung des historischen Stadtgrundrisses verband. Kleihues rehabilitierte bereits 1977 mit dem Block 270 am Vinetaplatz im Sanierungsgebiet Wedding Brunnenstraße die geschlossene Blockrandbebauung, die in der Vor- wie Nachkriegsmoderne als Inbegriff der sozialen Misere und der Spekulationsexzesse der Mietskasernenstadt des 19. Jahrhunderts galt.

Florian Wüst

excessive real estate speculation of the nineteenth-century tenement city. The framework plan for IBA's new construction areas, which Kleihues surprisingly made public in summer 1981, almost exclusively related to the perimeters defined by the street grid: a manifesto for the traditional European city.[14]

With his overarching concept, which also included rebuilding the areas near the Berlin Wall around Potsdamer Platz, Kleihues tackled the debates surrounding the Central Area. In order to secure the Senate's overall control, the senator for urban development and environmental protection, Volker Hassemer, who was appointed after the CDU won the spring 1981 elections, pushed ahead with the Central Area planning, which aimed to create a new means of incorporating the opinions of professionals.[15] Headed by a "core group," weekly discussions and conferences were held between May 1982 and May 1983; expert reports were also commissioned. Architects Ernst Jacoby, Volker Martin, and Karl Pächter represented a unique stance that integrated ecology and history into a concrete place. In their eyes, a lack of perspective for the city as a whole required a future in which spaces were not obstructed but kept clear. This took the form of provisionally designed green spaces and traffic routes: "A composition that merely designs the half-city's conditions as smoothly as possible, that suggests self-sufficiency with aesthetic means and denies contradiction, is an attitude even less historical than simply leaving things as they are, which at least provides the chance of remembrance."[16]

Given the many "talks and meetings without the authority to make decisions," initial enthusiasm soon waned; the attempt to organize the Central Area did not result in a proposal with broad political support, as was hoped.[17] Nevertheless, or perhaps precisely because of this, the process, including its published plans and collections of materials, succeeded in presenting the no-man's-land in the heart of the divided city as a highly charged area: "The specters of national history were now here for everyone to perceive."[18]

At the Gates

One of the heavily haunted places was the Prinz-Albrecht terrain, later officially renamed "Topography of Terror", a wasteland between the Martin-Gropius-Bau and Wilhelmstraße. Berlin's worst address: the Prinz-Albrecht-Palais and its neighboring buildings housed the Secret State Police (Gestapo) and the SS Security Service, as well as the Reich Security Main Office from 1939. After 1945, the remains of the buildings were completely demolished. When the site's history was finally made public, it had already been used for many years as a practice driving area and dumping site for rubble from the Kreuzberg redevelopment project. Riki Kalbe's experimental documentary *Ground Analysis* (*Bodenproben*; 1987), which dissects the treatment or non-treatment of the site with impressive clarity, explains that excavators "bury old destruction with the rubble of new destruction." On the occasion of Berlin's 750th anniversary in 1987, the foundations, the remnants of the torture cells, were uncovered and made accessible, with an exhibition to accompany it. This temporary structure remained in use until the opening of the new Topography of Terror Documentation Center in 2010.

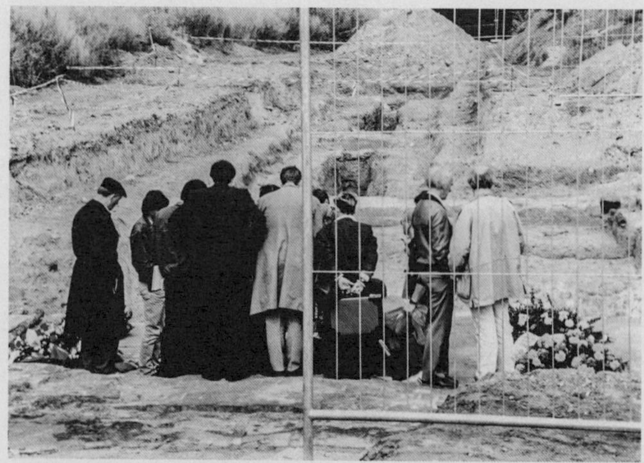

Bodenproben (*Ground Analysis*), Riki Kalbe, 1987 (film still).

So bezog sich der Rahmenplan für die IBA-Neubaugebiete, den Kleihues im Sommer 1981 überraschend publik machte, nahezu ausschließlich auf die durch das Straßenraster definierten Bebauungskanten: ein Manifest für die traditionelle europäische Stadt.[14]

Mit seinem Gesamtkonzept, das auch die Bebauung der mauernahen Gebiete rund um den Potsdamer Platz vorsah, grätschte Kleihues in die Diskussionen über den Zentralen Bereich. Um die Federführung des Senats zu sichern, forcierte der nach dem Wahlgewinn der CDU im Frühjahr 1981 eingesetzte Senator für Stadtentwicklung und Umweltschutz, Volker Hassemer, das Planungsverfahren Zentraler Bereich, welches auf neue Weise die Fachöffentlichkeit zu beteiligen beabsichtigte.[15] Gesteuert durch eine „Kerngruppe" fanden zwischen Mai 1982 und Mai 1983 wöchentliche Gesprächsrunden und Tagungen statt, Gutachten wurden in Auftrag gegeben. Eine bemerkenswerte Position, die Ökologie und Geschichte als konkreten Ort miteinander verbindet, vertraten die Architekten Ernst Jacoby, Volker Martin und Karl Pächter. Die fehlende Perspektive der Gesamtstadt gebiete es, die Zukunft nicht zu verbauen, sondern in Form provisorisch gestalteter Grünräume und Verkehrswege freizuhalten: „Eine Gestaltung, die nur die Bedingungen der Halbstadt möglichst glatt designt, die Autarkie mit ästhetischen Mitteln suggeriert und den Widerspruch leugnet – diese Einstellung ist noch geschichtsloser als das einfache Liegenlassen, das wenigsten die Chance der Erinnerung beläßt."[16]

Ob des vielen „Redens und Tagens ohne Beschlussvollmacht" verflog die anfängliche Begeisterung, der Versuch der räumlichen Ordnung des Zentralen Bereichs führte nicht zum erhofften, breit getragenen politischen Entwurf.[17] Dennoch oder vielleicht gerade deshalb vermochte das Verfahren samt seiner publizierten Konzepte und Materialsammlungen das Niemandsland im Herzen der geteilten Stadt als hochsensibles Gebiet zu deuten: „Hier spukten nunmehr für jeden spürbar die Geister der nationalen Geschichte."[18]

The city's anniversary spurred the renovation and cultural presentation of historic buildings on both sides of the Wall. In the East, the Nikolaiviertel was reconstructed; the Martin-Gropius-Bau in the West had already been renovated into a museum in 1981 and was now to be followed by the Hamburger Bahnhof. In keeping with the motto "At the gates of the city," the West Berlin events were mainly held in the Central Area. The metaphor of a gateway—already present in the summary of the Central Area planning process's concepts and objectives published in 1985—was reintroduced into the discussion. Potsdamer Platz was now conceived as "a space in transition, a modern form of the old wasteland 'at the gates.'"[19] Once the site of Potsdamer Tor, Potsdamer Platz was intersected by the Berliner Zoll- und Akzisemauer (Berlin Customs Wall) until the mid-nineteenth century. Now, the Berlin Wall crossed the middle of the city—but without any gate. To foster the normalization of intra-German relations, the Senate planners wished for a border crossing: a double gate rather than a double periphery. Studies for the renovation of Potsdamer Platz feature rows of trees and groves drawn in with a ruler. The Esplanade Filmhaus would have been located in between.

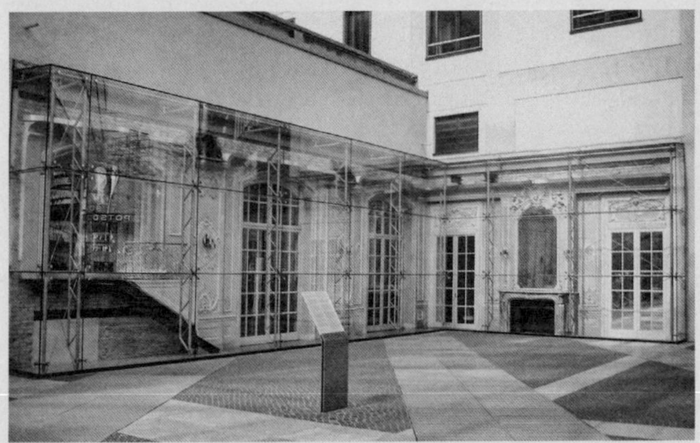

Fragment of the Esplanade breakfast room, Sony Center, 2006.

Berlin Tomorrow

In summer 1989, Daimler-Benz AG was searching West Berlin for a location for the headquarters of one of its subsidiaries, the service company Debis. The Senate offered them three sites within the Central Area, and the Stuttgart-based company chose Potsdamer Platz. The fall of the Berlin Wall coincided with these sale negotiations, and a few months later German reunification was set in stone. The desirability of the sixty thousand-square-meter site multiplied virtually overnight. Nevertheless, the Senate agreed to an unlawfully low sale price, hoping to attract further major investors. The contract was signed in summer 1990, and two years later Daimler-Benz had to make a light additional payment. On the other side of Potsdamer Straße, Sony was made a similar offer. However, the Senate succeeded in including the original Esplanade Filmhaus plans for the site into the new building complex, at least partially, as well as the parts of the hotel that had been listed in 1989. The final sale price, of around one hundred million deutsche marks, was lowered to include these

Vor den Toren

Einer der schwer spukenden Orte war die das Prinz-Albrecht-Gelände, später offiziell „Topographie des Terrors" genannte Brache zwischen Martin-Gropius-Bau und Wilhelmstraße. Berlins schlimmste Adresse: Im Prinz-Albrecht-Palais und dessen benachbarten Gebäuden waren die Geheime Staatspolizei (Gestapo) und der Sicherheitsdienst der SS, ab 1939 zudem das Reichssicherheitshauptamt untergebracht. Nach 1945 wurden sämtliche Häuserreste abgerissen. Als die Geschichte des Ortes endlich an die Öffentlichkeit drang, diente er bereits viele Jahre als Verkehrsübungsplatz und Schuttabladestelle für die Kreuzberger Sanierung. Bagger „verschütten Verwüstung mit den Trümmern neuer Verwüstung", erklärt Riki Kalbes experimenteller Dokumentarfilm *Bodenproben* (1987), der den Umgang beziehungsweise Nicht-Umgang mit dem Gelände in beeindruckender Klarheit seziert. Zur 750-Jahrfeier Berlins 1987 wurden die Fundamente, die Reste der Folterzellen, freigelegt und, ergänzt durch eine Ausstellung, zugänglich gemacht. Dieses Provisorium verblieb bis zur Eröffnung des neuen Dokumentationszentrums Topographie des Terrors im Jahr 2010.

Das Stadtjubiläum führte beiderseits der Mauer zur Renovierung und kulturellen Bespielung historischer Bauten. Im Osten wurde das Nikolaiviertel wiederaufgebaut, im Westen war der Martin-Gropius-Bau 1981 museal hergerichtet worden, nun folgte der Hamburger Bahnhof. Passend zum Motto „Vor den Toren der Stadt" fanden die Westberliner Veranstaltungen vorwiegend im Zentralen Bereich statt. Die Metapher des Torraums gebrauchte bereits die 1985 veröffentlichte Zusammenfassung der Konzepte und Ziele des Planungsverfahrens Zentraler Bereich, die erneut in die Diskussion eingebracht werden sollten. Als ein solcher war der Potsdamer Platz gedacht: „ein Raum im Übergang, eine moderne Form der alten Brache ‚vor den Toren'".[19] Einst Standort des Potsdamer Tores verlief hier bis zur Hälfte des 19. Jahrhunderts die Berliner Zoll- und Akzisemauer. Nun, mitten durch die Stadt, die Berliner Mauer – ohne Tor. Als Beitrag zur Normalisierung der innerdeutschen Beziehungen wünschten sich die Senatsplaner einen Grenzübergang: doppelter Torraum statt doppelte Peripherie. Die Studien zur Neuordnung des Potsdamer Platzes zeigen mit dem Lineal gezogene Baumreihen und Haine. Dazwischen hätte das Filmhaus Esplanade gestanden.

Berlin morgen

Als die Daimler-Benz AG im Sommer 1989 in West-Berlin nach einem Ort für den Hauptsitz einer ihrer Tochtergesellschaften, dem Dienstleistungsunternehmen Debis, suchte, bot der Senat drei Flächen innerhalb des Zentralen Bereichs an. Der Stuttgarter Konzern wählte den Potsdamer Platz. In die Kaufverhandlungen platzte die Maueröffnung, in wenigen Monaten war die deutsche Wiedervereinigung beschlossene Sache. Die Attraktivität des über 60.000 Quadratmeter großen Grundstücks vervielfachte sich quasi über Nacht. Trotzdem ließ sich der Senat auf einen rechtswidrig niedrigen Kaufpreis ein, erhoffte sich eine Signalwirkung für weitere Großinvestoren. Im Sommer 1990 wurde unterschrieben, zwei Jahre später musste Daimler-Benz sachte nachzahlen. Auf der anderen

Florian Wüst

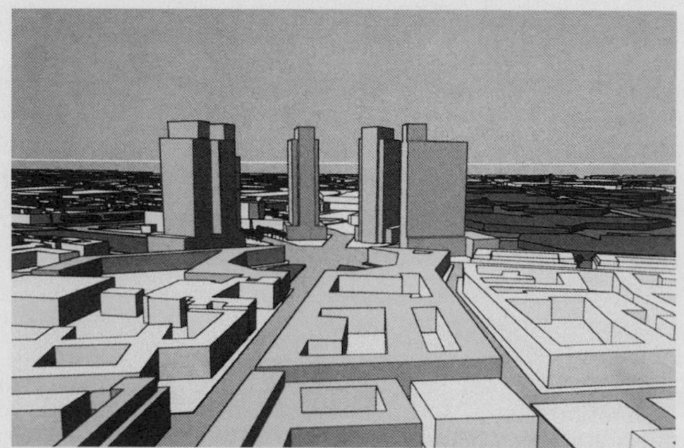

Hans Kollhoff, Leipziger Platz and Potsdamer Platz, digital draft, 1991.

expenses.[20] In a tremendous feat of engineering, the Kaisersaal was moved by around seventy meters. It was the only way it could fit into Helmut Jahn's architectural plan. Protected from the outside by glass walls, the Esplanade literally became a showcase. The institutions brought together under the Filmhaus roof were given the Sony Center's central section facing Potsdamer Straße. Here, the architect was only partially willing to adapt his extensive designs for an office building to the specific needs of a cinema, a museum, and a film school.

In early 1991, Frankfurt am Main's Deutsches Architekturmuseum and the *Frankfurter Allgemeine Zeitung* copresented the exhibition *Berlin Tomorrow*, bringing together ideas by internationally renowed architects for the redesign of Berlin's historic center, "which was suddenly up for grabs after the fall of the Wall."[21] Gifted visions for the metropolis of the future: "Mere architecture as art, without any proposals for the unification of Berlin from a perspective of practical life," as Bruno Flierl would later conclude.[22]

The debate over granting approval to high-rise buildings remained a point of contention, with a strong case made by Hans Kollhoff's designs for corresponding high-rise clusters at Potsdamer Platz and Alexanderplatz. Although the low-block structure by Hilmer & Sattler and Albrecht emerged victorious from the urban planning competition for Potsdamer Platz, whose jury Rem Koolhaas left in fury at the "terrible waste of an endeavor that was unique in Europe in the twentieth century,"[23] the investors insisted on adding towers to the western side of the "gateway area." Sony would ultimately completely ignore the urban planning specifications. Elsewhere, the doctrine of "critical reconstruction" advocated by Kleihues and Senate Building Director Hans Stimmann petrified the center of Berlin at eaves height. GDR modernism was torn down wherever possible. Not only Potsdamer Platz, but the entire center of East Berlin, from Friedrichstraße and Gendarmenmarkt to Alexanderplatz, was transformed into the "world's largest construction site" within a few years.[24]

The property sales at Potsdamer Platz were carried out without valid urban land-use permits. The investors built the streets and squares themselves and were granted domiciliary rights on top. The tenor of the criticism being voiced

Straßenseite der Potsdamer Straße kam Sony zu ähnlichen Bedingungen zum Zug. Wobei hier der Senat durchsetzte, die ursprüngliche Filmhaus Esplanade-Planung für das Grundstück zumindest ansatzweise sowie die 1989 unter Denkmalschutz gestellten Teile des Hotels in den neuen Gebäudekomplex zu integrieren. In den Kaufpreis von rund 100 Millionen Mark waren diese Aufwendungen verbilligend eingepreist.[20] Der Kaisersaal wurde in einem hanebüchenen technischen Kraftakt um etwa 70 Meter versetzt. Nur so passte er in Helmut Jahns Architektur. Nach außen von Glaswänden geschützt, landete das Esplanade buchstäblich in der Vitrine. Die unter dem Dach des Filmhauses zusammengeführten Institutionen erhielten den Mittelteil des Sony Centers zur Potsdamer Straße hin. Hier war der Architekt nur bedingt bereit, sein durchgestaltetes Bürohaus den spezifischen Bedarfen eines Kinos, eines Museums und einer Filmschule anzupassen.

Anfang 1991 hatte das Deutsche Architekturmuseum in Frankfurt am Main zusammen mit der Frankfurter Allgemeinen Zeitung die Ausstellung *Berlin morgen* gezeigt, die die Ideen international renommierter Architekt*innen zur Neugestaltung des historischen Zentrums von Berlin versammelte, „das nach dem Fall der Mauer auf einmal zur Disposition stand."[21] Geschenkte Visionen für die Metropole der Zukunft: „Bloße Architektur als Kunst, ohne Vorschläge zur Vereinigung Berlins vom praktischen Leben her", urteilt Bruno Flierl im Rückblick.[22] Hängen blieb die Debatte um das Ja oder Nein zu Hochhäusern, wofür sich Hans Kollhoffs Entwurf korrespondierender Hochhaus-Cluster am Potsdamer Platz und am Alexanderplatz starkmachte. Obwohl aus dem städtebaulichen Wettbewerb zum Potsdamer Platz, dessen Jury Rem Koolhaas wütend verließ, ob der „schreckliche[n] Vergeudung einer im 20. Jahrhundert europaweit einzigartigen Unternehmung"[23], die niedrige Blockstruktur von Hilmer & Sattler und Albrecht siegreich hervorging, ließen es sich die Investoren nicht nehmen, die westliche Seite des „Torraums" mit Türmen zu bestücken. Sony ignorierte die städtebaulichen Vorgaben sogar ganz. Andernorts versteinerte die von Kleihues und Senatsbaudirektor Hans Stimmann vertretene Doktrin der kritischen Rekonstruktion das Berliner Zentrum in Traufhöhe. DDR-Moderne wurde abgerissen, wo es ging. Nicht nur der Potsdamer Platz, die ganze Ostberliner Mitte, Friedrichstraße, Gendarmenmarkt bis zum Alexanderplatz, verwandelte sich innerhalb weniger Jahre in die „größte Baustelle der Welt"[24].

Die Grundstücksverkäufe am Potsdamer Platz waren ohne gültige Bauleitplanung erfolgt. Straßen und Plätze errichteten die Investoren selbst, das Hausrecht dafür bekamen sie obendrauf. Die mit dem Zusammenwachsen aus dem Stand überforderte Stadt hätte durch die Privatisierung öffentlichen Bodens den politischen Gestaltungswillen abgegeben, lautete der Tenor der Kritik: „Investorenglück vor Gemeinwohl."[25] Die „Chance der Erinnerung", die Architekturgeschichte nicht einfach zitiert und postmodern transformiert, blies der neoliberale Umbau weg wie den Sand von der „arischen Trümmerwüste des Dritten Reiches". So der Wortlaut in Hito Steyerls Essayfilm *Die leere Mitte* (1998), der Geschichtsvergessenheit und neue Grenzziehungen im wiedervereinigten Deutschland am Beispiel der Umgebung des Potsdamer Platzes aufzeigt. Die von Steyerl beobachteten, handgreiflich rassistischen Demonstrationen von Gewerkschaftler*innen gegen die Billiglohnarbeiter aus der Fremde,

was that the city, overburdened with the task of growing together from a standing position, had surrendered its political will to shape the future through the privatization of public land: "Investor happiness before the common good."[25] The "opportunity for remembrance," which goes beyond simply quoting architectural history and transforming it in a postmodern manner, was blown away by neoliberal reconstruction like sands from the "Aryan ruins of the Third Reich"—as Hito Steyerl's essay film *The Empty Center* (*Die leere Mitte*; 1998) phrases it. Through the example of Potsdamer Platz, the film illustrates how history was forgotten and new boundaries were drawn in reunified Germany. Steyerl's camera observes violent racist demonstrations by trade unionists against the low-wage workers from abroad who toiled on Berlin's construction sites, which today seem like harbingers of the current social climate in the country.

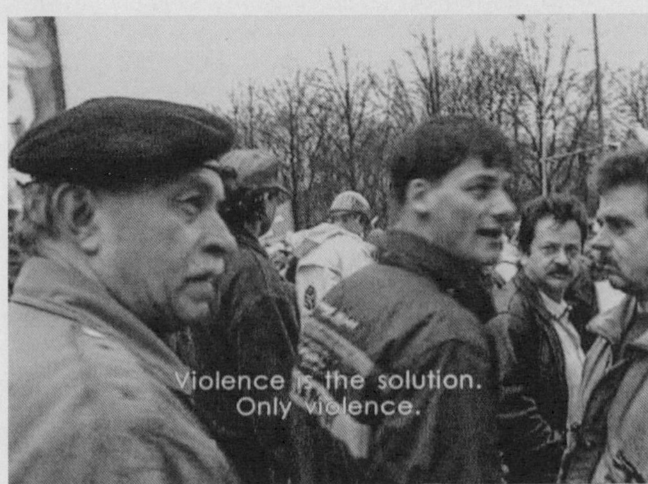

Die leere Mitte (*The Empty Center*), Hito Steyerl, 1998 (film still).

So, the Filmhaus at Potsdamer Platz will soon be history. Arsenal first arrived here from Schöneberg's Welserstraße; after a nomadic year in 2025, it will move into the longtime site of its archive and screening rooms: silent green in Wedding, i.e., in the vicinity of the Harun Farocki Institute, transmediale, Sinema Transtopia, and SAVVY Contemporary. In the long interim, it has drawn its audience to the cinema "not because of, but in spite of Potsdamer Platz."[26] DFFB will relocate to Adlershof, until their future spaces at Berlin Decks are completed, an innovation campus in Moabit above Europacity, which continues the legacy of the capitalized city in the northern part of the Central Area. And the Deutsche Kinemathek and its film museum will find a temporary home in the E-Werk between Wilhelmstraße and Mauerstraße—trusting that the new, publicly owned Filmhaus will indeed be built in the parking lot next to the Gropius Bau, which it will then occupy together with the Berlinale rather than the Arsenal and the DFFB.[27]

At the end of *Wings of Desire*, Cassiel sits atop the Victory Column on the Große Stern roundabout. If he sat on the top of the city today and looked down, he would probably still hear the old narrator's voice in his head: "For they need me ... more than anything in the world."

die auf den Berliner Baustellen schufteten, wirken wie Vorboten des aktuellen gesellschaftlichen Klimas im Land.

Am Potsdamer Platz ist das Filmhaus also bald Geschichte. Das Arsenal kam aus der Schöneberger Welserstraße und wird sich nach einem nomadischen Jahr 2025 dorthin begeben, wo sich bereits seit längerem Archiv und Sichtungsräume befinden: ins Weddinger silent green und damit in die Nachbarschaft von Harun Farocki Institut, transmediale, Sinema Transtopia oder SAVVY Contemporary. In der langen Zwischenzeit musste es sein Publikum „nicht wegen, sondern trotz des Potsdamer Platzes"[26] ins Kino holen. Die DFFB zieht nach Adlershof, bis ihre zukünftigen Räume in den Berlin Decks fertiggestellt sind, einem Innovationscampus in Moabit, oberhalb der Europacity, die im nördlichen Teil des Zentralen Bereichs die Geschichte der kapitalisierten Stadt fortschreibt. Und die Deutsche Kinemathek samt Filmmuseum findet im E-Werk zwischen Wilhelmstraße und Mauerstraße einen temporären Unterschlupf – darauf vertrauend, dass das neue, dann in öffentlicher Hand befindliche Filmhaus auf dem Parkplatz neben dem Gropius Bau wirklich gebaut wird, welches nicht mit Arsenal und DFFB, sondern gemeinsam mit der Berlinale bezogen werden soll.[27]

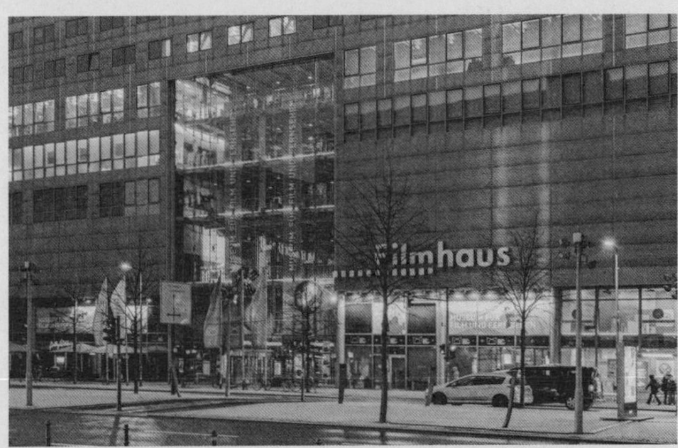

The Filmhaus's façade, Sony Center, January 2014.

Am Ende von *Der Himmel über Berlin* sitzt Cassiel alleine oben auf der Siegessäule am Großen Stern. Säße er heute auf den Spitzen der Stadt und sähe hinab, hätte er wohl unverändert den alten Erzähler im Ohr: „Weil sie mich brauchen, wie sonst nichts auf der Welt."

Florian Wüst

1   Wolfgang Kil, "Im Niemandsland," in *Gründerparadise. Vom Bauen in Zeiten des Übergangs* (Berlin: Bauwesen, 2000), 32.
2   The Japanese Sony Group sold the Sony Center to the real estate investment companies Oxford Properties and Madison International Realty in 2017. In July 2022, Norges Bank Investment Management acquired 44.9 percent of Oxford's stake and the entire 5.1 percent from Madison. In conjunction with the comprehensive modernization of the building complex, which was completed in 2000, it was provisionally renamed Center am Potsdamer Platz. The final new name is to be announced in 2024. Cf. "Oxford Properties and Norges Bank rename Berlin's Sony Center as part of €200 million repositioning," News, Oxford Properties, March 4, 2023, https://www.oxfordproperties.com/news/oxford-properties-and-norges-bank-rename-berlins-sony-center-as-part-of-200-million-repositioning-.
3   Andreas Busche, "Entsteht ein zentrales Filmhaus für Berlin?," *Tagesspiegel*, May 15, 2017.
4   Today known as Arsenal – Institute for Film and Video Art.
5   Cf. "Wettbewerb Filmhaus Esplanade, Berlin," *DBZ Deutsche Bauzeitung*, no. 9, 1986, 1056.
6   Cf. Hans Helmut Prinzler, "Der Mythos des Niemandslands," interview by Gerhard Midding, *der Freitag*, September 29, 2000.
7   "Entscheidung für Berliner Filmhaus," *taz*, October 27, 1990.
8   Harun Farocki, "Ich habe genug!," *Biedermann und die Brandstifter, Les Choses. Berliner Hefte zur Architektur*, no. 1, 1985, 62 et seq. (translated by Lisa Contag).
9   Dieter Hoffmann-Axthelm, "Berliner Zentrum," *Stadtbauwelt 72, Bauwelt*, no. 48, 1981, 2175.
10   It was not only after the end of World War II that parts of the Potsdamer Platz area lay derelict. From 1937 onwards, entire streets of the Friedrichsvorstadt fell victim to Albert Speer's plans for Berlin as the capital of the Third Reich, and the upper-class apartment buildings and villas between Tiergarten and the Landwehr Canal, including many owned by Jewish families, were ruthlessly expropriated and demolished.
11   Hoffmann-Axthelm, "Berliner Zentrum," 2176 (translated by Lisa Contag).
12   Ibid., 2177.
13   Cf. Krijn Thijs, "West-Berliner Visionen für eine neue Mitte. Die Internationale Bauausstellung, der 'Zentrale Bereich' und die 'Geschichtslandschaft'an der Mauer (1981–1985)," *Zeithistorische Forschungen/Studies in Contemporary History*, no. 11, 2014, 23 et seq.
14   Cf. Josef Paul Kleihues, "Sieben Essentials zum Rahmenplan für die Neubaugebiete der Internationalen Bauausstellung Berlin," *Stadtbauwelt 71, Bauwelt*, no. 36, 1981, 1589–95.
15   Cf. Hanno Klein, "Das Planungsverfahren Zentraler Bereich, Grundlagen und Ziele," *Die räumliche Ordnung des Zentralen Bereichs. Entwicklungsgrundlagen und Konzepte*, Schriften dès Senators für Stadtentwicklung und Umweltschutz zum Zentralen Bereich, no. 1, 1985, 15 et seq.
16   Ernst Jacoby, Volker Martin, Karl Pächter, "Der Zentrale Bereich an der Nahtstelle von Ost und West braucht keine endgültige ästhetische Lösung – West, sondern ein gestaltetes Provisorium, Berlin, Oktober 1982,"

1   Wolfgang Kil, „Im Niemandsland" [1995], in: Ders., *Gründerparadise. Vom Bauen in Zeiten des Übergangs*, Berlin 2000, S. 32.
2   Der japanische Elektronikkonzern Sony verkaufte das Sony Center 2017 an die Immobilien-Investmentgesellschaften Oxford Properties Group und Madison International Realty. Im Juli 2022 übernahm Norges Bank Investment Management 44,9 Prozent des Oxford-Anteils sowie die gesamten 5,1 Prozent von Madison. Verbunden mit der umfassenden Modernisierung des im Jahr 2000 fertiggestellten Gebäudekomplexes erfolgte die vorläufige Umbenennung in „Center am Potsdamer Platz". Der endgültige neue Name soll noch in 2024 bekanntgegeben werden. Vgl. Oxfordproperties.com, 03.04.2023, https://www.oxfordproperties.com/news/oxford-properties-and-norges-bank-rename-berlins-sony-center-as-part-of-200-million-repositioning- (letzter Zugriff: 03.04.2024).
3   Andreas Busche, „Entsteht ein zentrales Filmhaus für Berlin?", in: *Der Tagesspiegel*, 15.05.2017.
4   Heute: Arsenal – Institut für Film und Videokunst.
5   Vgl. „Wettbewerb Filmhaus Esplanade, Berlin", in: *DBZ Deutsche Bauzeitung*, Heft 9, 1986, S. 1056.
6   Vgl. „Der Mythos des Niemandslands", Hans Helmut Prinzler im Gespräch mit Gerhard Midding, in: *der Freitag*, 29.09.2000.
7   „Entscheidung für Berliner Filmhaus", in: *taz*, 27.10.1990.
8   Harun Farocki, „Ich habe genug!", in: *Biedermann und die Brandstifter*, Les Choses. *Berliner Hefte zur Architektur*, Heft 1, 1985, S. 62 f.
9   Dieter Hoffmann-Axthelm, „Berliner Zentrum", in: *Stadtbauwelt 72*, Bauwelt, Heft 48, 1981, S. 2175.
10   Nicht erst nach Ende des Zweiten Weltkriegs lag die Gegend des Potsdamer Platzes in Teilen brach. Albert Speers Plänen für Berlin als Hauptstadt des Dritten Reiches waren ab 1937 ganze Straßenzüge der Friedrichsvorstadt zum Opfer gefallen, die großbürgerlichen Mietshäuser und Villen zwischen Tiergarten und Landwehrkanal, darunter viel Besitz jüdischer Familien, rücksichtslos enteignet und abgerissen worden.
11   Hoffmann-Axthelm (wie Anm. 9), S. 2176.
12   Ebd., S. 2177.
13   Vgl. Krijn Thijs, „West-Berliner Visionen für eine neue Mitte. Die Internationale Bauausstellung, der »Zentrale Bereich« und die »Geschichtslandschaft« an der Mauer (1981–1985)", in: *Zeithistorische Forschungen/Studies in Contemporary History*, Heft 11, 2014, S. 237 f.
14   Vgl. Josef Paul Kleihues, „Sieben Essentials zum Rahmenplan für die Neubaugebiete der Internationalen Bauausstellung Berlin", in: *Stadtbauwelt 71*, Bauwelt, Heft 36, 1981, S. 1589–1595.
15   Vgl. Hanno Klein, „Das Planungsverfahren Zentraler Bereich, Grundlagen und Ziele", in: *Die räumliche Ordnung des Zentralen Bereichs. Entwicklungsgrundlagen und Konzepte*, Schriften des Senators für Stadtentwicklung und Umweltschutz zum Zentralen Bereich, Heft 1, Berlin 1985, S. 15 f.
16   Ernst Jacoby, Volker Martin, Karl Pächter, „Der Zentrale Bereich an der Nahtstelle von Ost und West braucht keine endgültige ästhetische Lösung – West, sondern ein gestaltetes Provisorium, Berlin, Oktober 1982", in: *Dokumentation zum Planungsverfahren Zentraler Bereich, Mai*

Dokumentation zum Planungsverfahren Zentraler Bereich, Mai 1982 – Mai 1983, ed. Senator für Stadtentwicklung und Umweltschutz, Berlin 1983, 171 (translated by Lisa Contag). Speaking of "leaving things as they are": the irony of urban progress lies in the fact that in the Central Area nature was able to take over spaces abandoned by people for decades, providing present-day Berlin's unique post-industrial park landscapes. Traffic planning that privileged cars also set out to cut up the old city. The section of the city highway known as the Westtangente was originally intended to run from Schöneberger Kreuz along the route of the S1 via Gleisdreieck to Kemperplatz, where it dipped into the Tiergarten tunnel, which was only built thirty years later. The asphalt road through the middle of Berlin's center never came, not least because of the persistent protests of the Westtangente Citizens' Initiative founded in 1974. However, many of the areas that had been set aside for the project remained free of development.

17   Thijs, "West-Berliner Visionen," 246 et seq. (translated by Lisa Contag).
18   Ibid., 250 (translated by Lisa Contag).
19   Edvard Jahn, "Konzepte zur räumlichen Ordnung," *Die räumliche Ordnung des Zentralen Bereichs. Entwicklungs-grundlagen und Konzepte*, Schriften des Senators für Stadtentwicklung und Umweltschutz zum Zentralen Bereich, no. 1, 1985, 68.
20   Cf. Ole/Roda, "Grabungsarbeiten für High-Tech," *taz*, September 9, 1995.
21   Vittorio Magnago Lampugnani and Michael Mönninger, "Vorwort," in *Berlin morgen. Ideen für das Herz der Groszstadt*, ed. Vittorio Magnago Lampugnani and Michael Mönninger (Stuttgart: G. Hatje, 1991), 7 (translated by Lisa Contag).
22   Bruno Flierl, "Hauptstadtplanung im geteilten und vereinten Berlin," in *Berlin plant. Plädoyer für ein Planwerk Innenstadt Berlin 2.0*, ed. Harald Bodenschatz and Thomas Flierl (Berlin: Verlag Theater der Zeit, 2010), 58.
23   Michael Mönninger and Hans Stimmann, "Es ist dramatisch, in der Mitte eine Leere zu haben," interviewed by Arno Brandlhuber and Florian Hertweck, in *The Dialogic City — Berlin wird Berlin*, ed. Arno Brandlhuber, Florian Hertweck, and Thomas Mayfried (Cologne: Verlag der Buchhandlung Walther König, 2015),140 (translated by Lisa Contag).
24   Cf. "Die größte Baustelle der Welt," *Der Spiegel*, July 19, 1992.
25   Heinrich Wefing, "Berliner Binnenkolonisation. Nachrichten aus einem berührten Land," in Andreas Muhs and Heinrich Wefing, *Der neue Potsdamerplatz. Ein Kunststück Stadt*, (Berlin: be.bra Verlag, 1998), 44 (translated by Lisa Contag).
26   As stated by Birgit Kohler during a press and publicity conference at the future Kino Arsenal in the Westhalle of silent green, February 22, 2024 (translated by Lisa Contag).
27   Cf. Rainer Rother, "60. Geburtstag der Deutschen Kinemathek: 'Der Neubau eines Filmmuseums ist politisch gewollt,'" interviewed by Andreas Busche, *Tagesspiegel,* May 12, 2023.

1982 – Mai 1983, hrsg. vom Senator für Stadtentwicklung und Umweltschutz, Berlin 1983, S. 171. Apropos „Liegenlassen": In der Tatsache, dass die Stadtnatur im Zentralen Bereich über Jahrzehnte von Menschen verlassene Räume einnehmen und dem heutigen Berlin einzigartige postindustrielle Parklandschaften bescheren konnte, liegt die Ironie urbaner Fortschrittsgeschichte: Auch die autogerechte Verkehrsplanung machte sich daran, die alte Stadt zu zerschneiden. Das als Westtangente bezeichnete Teilstück der Stadtautobahn sollte vom Schöneberger Kreuz entlang der Trasse der S1 über das Gleisdreieck bis zum Kemperplatz führen und dort in den 30 Jahre später wirklich gebauten Tiergartentunnel abtauchen. Die Asphaltpiste mitten durch die Mitte kam nie, nicht zuletzt aufgrund des beharrlichen Protests der 1974 gegründeten Bürgerinitiative Westtangente. Viele der freigehaltenen Flächen aber blieben.

17   Thijs (wie Anm. 13), S. 246 f.
18   Ebd., S. 250.
19   Edvard Jahn, „Konzepte zur räumlichen Ordnung", in: *Die räumliche Ordnung des Zentralen Bereichs* (wie Anm. 15), S. 68.
20   Vgl. Ole/Roda, „Grabungsarbeiten für High-Tech", in: *taz*, 09.09.1995.
21   Vittorio Magnago Lampugnani, Michael Mönninger, „Vorwort", in: *Berlin morgen. Ideen für das Herz der Groszstadt*, hrsg. von Dies., Stuttgart 1991, S. 7.
22   Bruno Flierl, „Hauptstadtplanung im geteilten und vereinten Berlin", in: *Berlin plant. Plädoyer für ein Planwerk Innenstadt Berlin 2.0*, hrsg. von Harald Bodenschatz, Thomas Flierl, Berlin 2010, S. 58.
23   „Es ist dramatisch, in der Mitte eine Leere zu haben", Michael Mönninger und Hans Stimmann im Gespräch mit Arno Brandlhuber und Florian Hertweck [19.03.2015], in: *The Dialogic City — Berlin wird Berlin*, hrsg. von Dies., Thomas Mayfried, Köln 2015, S. 140.
24   Vgl. „Die größte Baustelle der Welt", in: *Der Spiegel*, 19.07.1992.
25   Heinrich Wefing, „Berliner Binnenkolonisation. Nachrichten aus einem berührten Land", in: Andreas Muhs, Ders., *Der neue Potsdamerplatz. Ein Kunststück Stadt*, Berlin 1998, S. 44.
26   Aussage von Birgit Kohler während des Branchen- und Presseempfangs im zukünftigen Kino Arsenal, Westhalle des silent green, 22.02.2024.
27   Vgl. „60. Geburtstag der Deutschen Kinemathek: ‚Der Neubau eines Filmmuseums ist politisch gewollt'", Rainer Rother im Gespräch mit Andreas Busche, in: *Der Tagesspiegel,* 12.05.2023.

Florian Wüst is a Berlin-based film curator and publisher. He has curated film programs and exhibitions for international art institutions, cinemas, and festivals. In 2021 he participated in *Time Without End*, the first exhibition of Fluentum's *In Medias Res* series. Wüst is cofounder of *Berlin Journals—On the History and Present State of the City*, which addresses social, cultural, and economic changes in Berlin and other cities.

In Medias Res #3: Postproductions
is the third and final issue of
a publication series published on
the occasion of the program series
In Medias Res: Media, (Still) Moving
(2021–24), at Fluentum, Berlin.

Editors
Dennis Brzek, Junia Thiede

Contributors
Loretta Fahrenholz
Richard Hawkins
Thomas Helbig
Margaret Honda
Evelyn Kreutzer
Elisa R. Linn
D'Ette Nogle
Maya Schweizer
Richard Sides
Mike Terry
Peter Wächtler
Florian Wüst

Translation
Lisa Contag

Copyediting
Andrew Wagner (English)
Karolin Meunier (German)

Proofreading
Andrew Wagner (English)
Dennis Brzek, Junia Thiede (German)

Graphic Design
HIT

Image Editing
Falk Messerschmidt

Cover Typography
Hanna Solf, Anne Marie Piguet
(from Bea Schlingelhoff:
Women Against Hitler)

Cover Images
Front:
Excerpt of the film script for
materialoutpost by D'Ette Nogle, 2021

Back:
Tom Cruise by Peter Wächtler, 2005

Published and distributed by
Mousse Publishing
Contrappunto s.r.l.
Via Pier Candido Decembrio 28,
20137, Milan–Italy
moussemagazine.it

First edition: 2024

Printed in Germany by
Druckerei Rüss, Potsdam

ISBN 978-88-6749-531-3

€8 / $10

© 2024 Fluentum, Mousse Publishing,
the artists, and the authors of the
texts

Fluentum

Founder and Director
Markus Hannebauer

Artistic Director
Junia Thiede

Curator
Dennis Brzek

Curatorial Assistant
Elisa Tinterri

Communication and Outreach
Katharine Spatz

Head of Production
Jörg Adam

A/V Technology
Moritz Hirsch

Fluentum
Clayallee 174
14195 Berlin
www.fluentum.org

Image Credits
(unless otherwise noted):
p.4, background: © H.R. Giger,
courtesy Martin Walz; bottom:
© Troma Entertainment
p.8, photo: Björn Zielaskowski
pp.18–23, photo: Stefan Korte
p.30, donation to the Arsenal –
Institute for Film and Video Art from
the private collection of Heiner Roß.
p.31, photo: Margaret Nissen,
© Stiftung Berliner Mauer
p.32, photo © Cynthia Beatt
p.33, photo © Geoportal Berlin /
Luftbilder 1984 / Schrägaufnahmen.
p.34, from Josef Paul Kleihues,
"Sieben Essentials zum Rahmenplan
für die Neubaugebiete der Internationalen Bauausstellung Berlin,"
Stadtbauwelt 71, Bauwelt, no.36, 1981.
p.35, photo © Cynthia Beatt
p.37, photo © Andreas Steinhoff
p.38, from *Berlin morgen. Ideen für das
Herz der Groszstadt*, ed. Vittorio
Magnago Lampugnani and Michael
Mönninger (Stuttgart: G. Hatje, 1991).
© Prof. Hans Kollhoff
p.39, photo © Marian Stefanowski
p.44, courtesy Richard Hawkins and
Greene Naftali, New York.
pp.48, 51, 52, photo: Stefan Korte

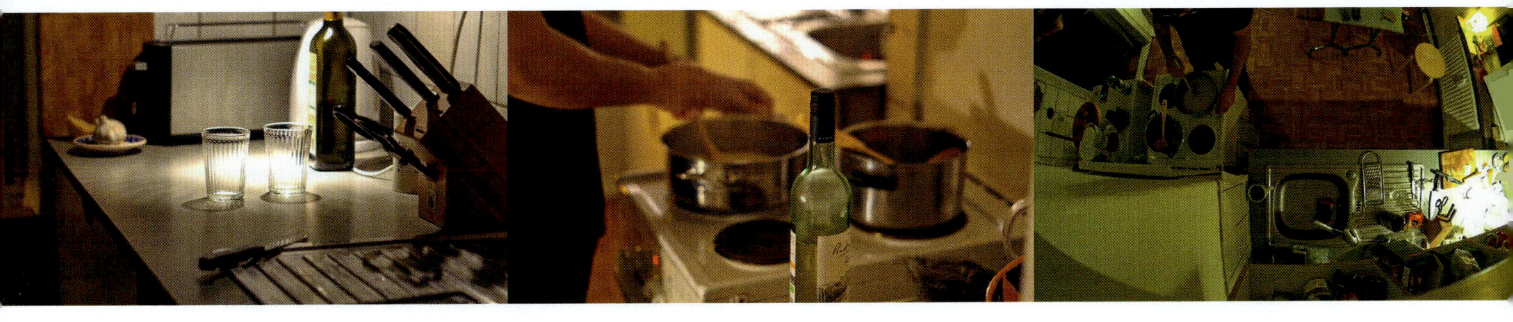

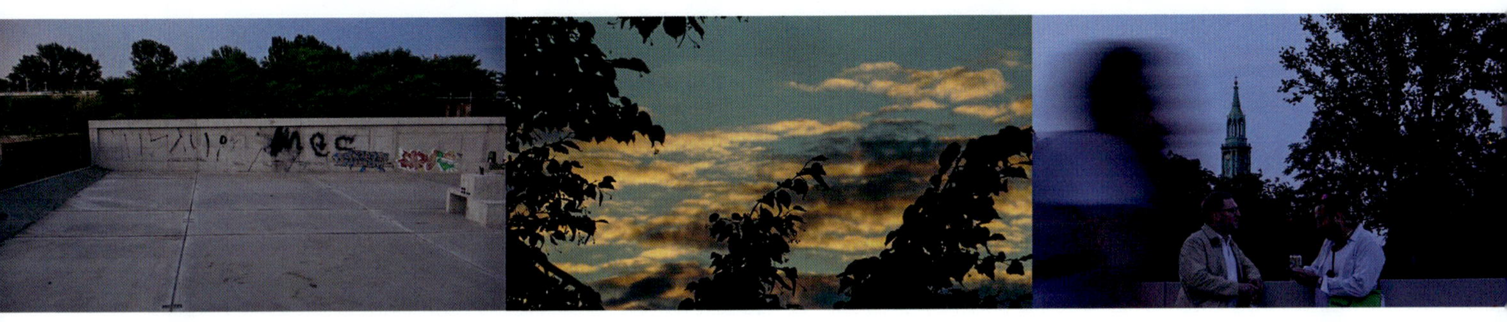

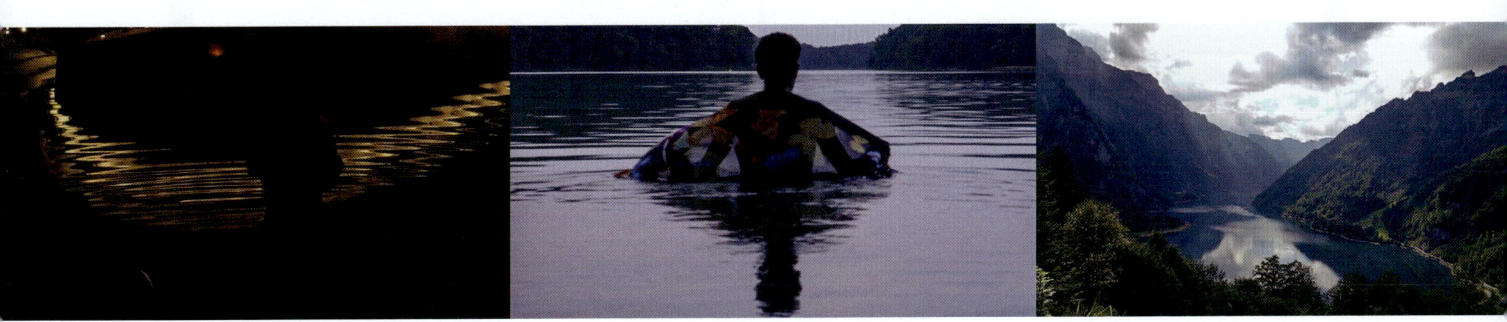

Richard Sides

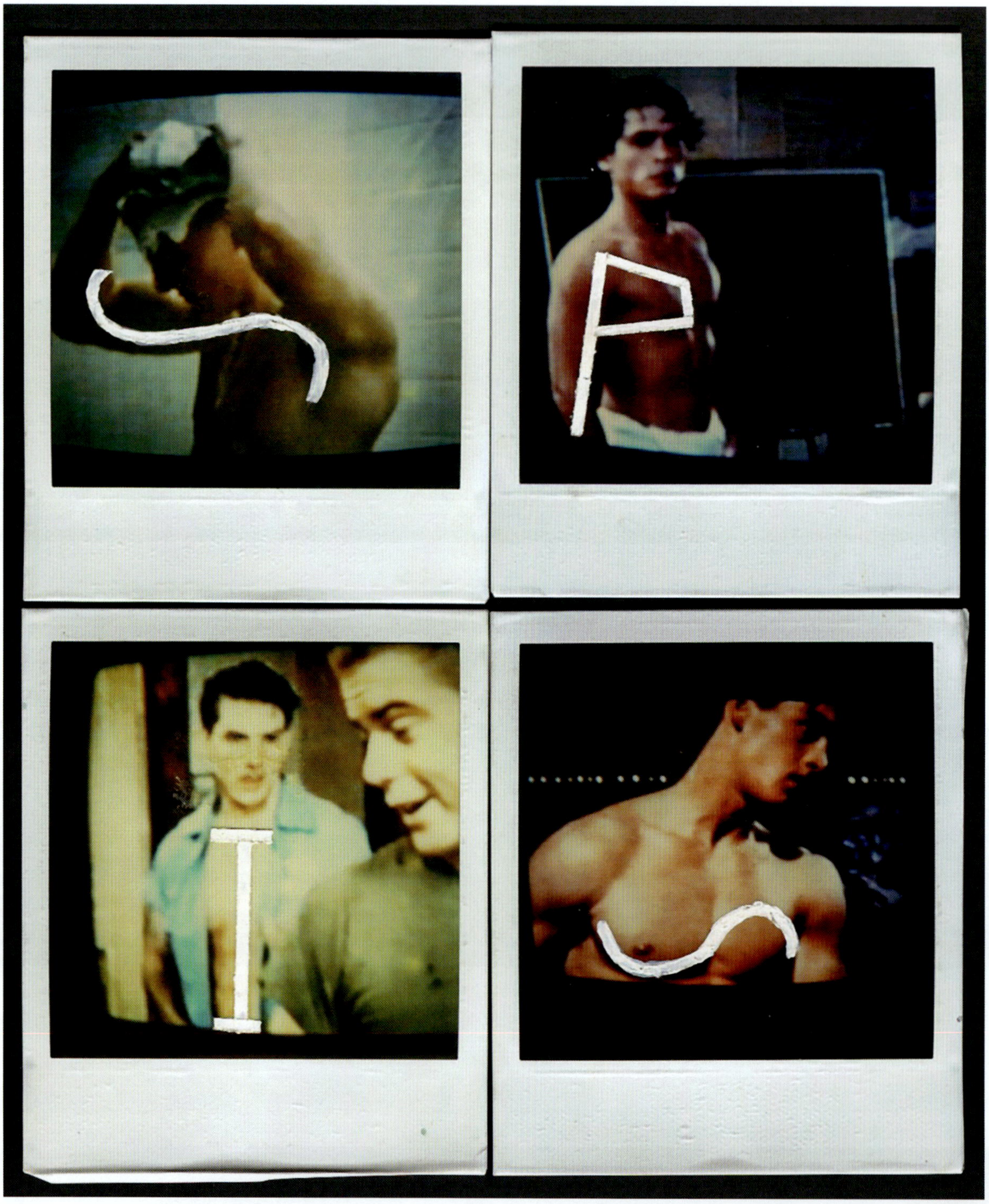

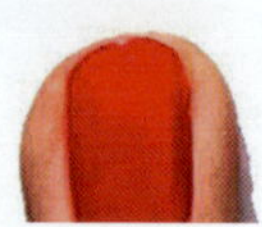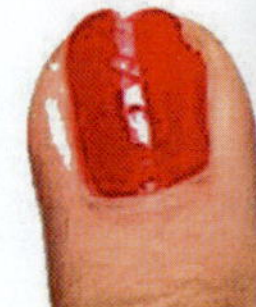

Richard Hawkins, *SPIS*, 1987
Acrylic on four Polaroids

Chapter four

Tom Cruise

The next morning the set is completely changed and the number of trailers more than doubled. It is the 20th of July. The set has been entirely reinstalled on a huge asphalted square. A wide meadow separates the square from the actual landing field. The location is a leftover of the Russian army, which held an airport in the area until 1994. The numerous new trailers shine white and glossy in the morning sun. They have arrived as part of the first unit equipment together with a huge canteen tent, a bigger catering truck with an American crew and a big tent with cooling systems for the extras, featuring numerous washing machines for their clothes. Seibi has heard the rumor that the tents are constantly held at 22,6 degrees, which would be, according to scientology rules, the best temperature for the human brain to function. Inside all the costumes are hanging on clothes lines, they are still moist from the nighttime laundry. Due to the white plastic foil, the light is shadeless, monotone and grey. It smells of washing powder. In one corner there are the hairdressers and make-up people installing a new work place. They sort out combs, tubes, flasks, brushes and the hair gel. On the other end of the tent the British costume crew goes about its business.

29

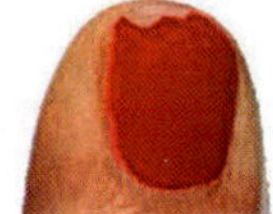

The guns are handed out, the props truck parks in the middle of the square. With no schedule given, I stroll down towards the landing field, towards the two fighting planes parked side by side. They are camouflaged with green, grey and black paint. One of the Swiss pilots polishes a plane and pauses to wipe the sweat off his forehead. Tom Cruise sits in the other plane, looking out the opened cockpit with glittering golden Ray-Ban glasses, smiling and waving at me. This makes me nervous. Already in full uniform, with my gun in my hands, I do not know where to go. I turn around and march straight off, back to the others, back to our Scientology tent, where I lay down underneath a bench, in-between the overhanging costumes and fall asleep.

In these minutes of light sleep I could have dreamt about all the lousy dinners in smoky kitchens to come, surrounded by friends or half friends, giving out this anecdote, combining it with witty remarks on Top Gun sequels grasping for awkward combinations of history to create the unforgettable laughter of a remarkable evening. These dreams would have been in line with Olaf's anecdote of Steven Seagal ordering pizza for everybody of the crew and sharing booze at a remote world war set, where the catering had been cancelled. But on the other hand: You have to know I come from a family where celebrities play no role. Admiration is more reserved for scientific achievements and yes, it's for the efforts. There are no stars. The few there are, are either dead or half-dead. Occasionally meeting Günther Grass in the Regional Express inbetween Lübeck and Hamburg, swimming with an aged Armin Müller Stahl in the same summery Baltic Sea, that's it. There are a few moderate anecdotes of almost having been seated close to someone well known at seldomly attended public gatherings.

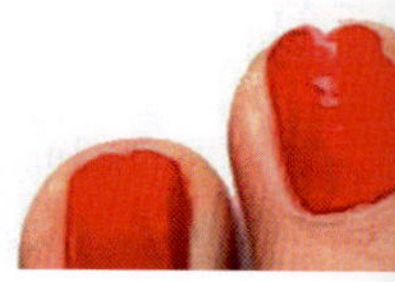

But these anecdotes are meant to be kept inside as a silent reward for a discipline full of privation, which is constantly needed to maintain one's most inner core. Autonomy. I could have dreamt that this maintenance would come to a stop and that this core would finally fall apart to be never, never, never put together again. I could have dreamt about all this, but I dreamt about something else, helicopters were involved and special forces.

31

Peter Wächtler

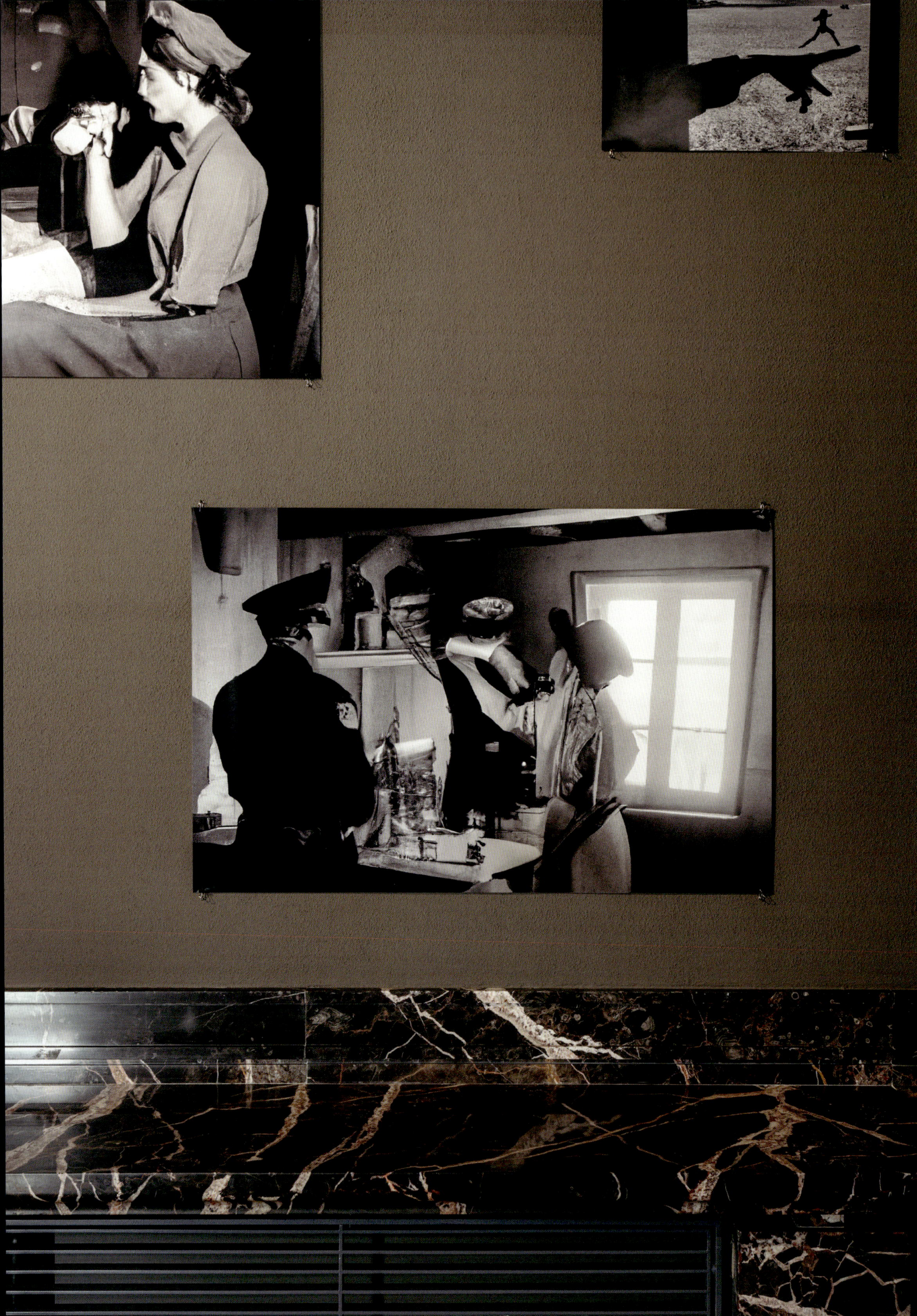

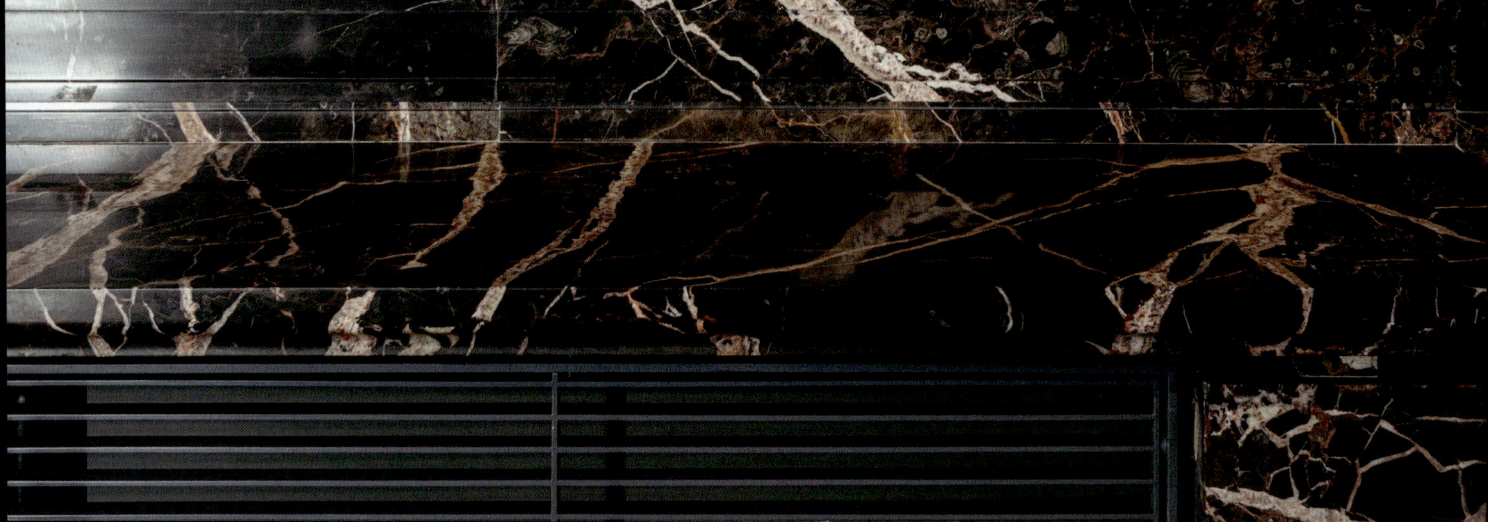

Evelyn Kreutzer
Inglourious Basterds and the Problem with History

The climax of Quentin Tarantino's *Inglourious Basterds* (2009), taking place shortly before the ending, provides spectacular images of two simultaneous vendettas against Hitler, carried out independently by Jewish-American soldiers and Jewish-French resistance fighters. In quick succession, we see film reels ablaze, movie theater seats in flames, a panicked audience stumbling over one another as they desperately flee, people firing machine guns at each other. The backdrop to this furor is a burning movie screen depicting a woman proclaiming revolt against Hitler and fascism ... Of course, this staged event never actually happened. It is precisely this lack of adherence to historical facts that makes *Inglourious Basterds* both compelling and problematic. How is this fictionalized assassination of Hitler to be understood as a cinematic act?

I would like to examine the film through two perspectives. The first is from a transatlantic lens: How might the film's interpretation change when seen from an American or German point of view? Such a consideration is particularly fitting for the context of Fluentum, which is housed in a building constructed by the Nazis and subsequently used by the US military following 1945; the American consulate is still next door today. It also served as a filming location for *Inglourious Basterds*, which was otherwise largely shot on the nearby Studio Babelsberg backlot. The second question I would like to address is to what extent *Inglourious Basterds* can be considered a film about films. It is a film that largely takes place in a cinema, foregrounds cinema operators and filmmakers, and deploys a visual and sonic language that evokes a myriad of eras and styles from film history.

And yet, it is not easy for me to write this text. I have ambivalent feelings and thoughts about both the hype surrounding director Quentin Tarantino and the film *Inglourious Basterds* itself. This is in part due to Tarantino's typical cartoonish usage of excessive violence. *Inglourious Basterds* unfolds via the director's trademark "loose" manner, but here in the context of the real historical trauma of the Holocaust rather than a purely fictional narrative. Furthermore, the film's plot is inflected by a counterfactual attitude that decisively rewrites the history of the Second World War as it follows two parallel plans to assassinate Hitler, which never existed in reality. All of this is told through an eclectic pastiche of various genres and stylistic devices from both avant-garde and "mainstream" Hollywood cinema. In turn, one could argue that the film contains a political message that is less concerned with the Holocaust than with its representation in the moving image.

When I first saw this film as a student shortly after its release, I was very affected and moved by some scenes, particularly the opening sequence in which the young French Jew Shosanna Dreyfus witnesses the slaughtering of her entire family by a Nazi general. However, the way Tarantino framed his story felt immoral: his continual tonal switching between thriller and comedy transformed the context of the Second World War and the Holocaust into more of an entertaining backdrop than the main subject matter. Upon rewatching the film, I noticed that it contained

Evelyn Kreutzer
Inglourious Basterds und das Problem mit der Geschichte

Der narrative Höhepunkt in Quentin Tarantinos *Inglourious Basterds* (2009), kurz vor Ende des Films, bietet spektakuläre Bilder zweier paralleler Rachefeldzüge gegen Hitler, ausgeübt von jüdisch-amerikanischen Soldaten und jüdisch-französischen Widerstandskämpfer*innen. Wir sehen brennende Filmrollen, brennende Kinositze, Menschen, die in Panik übereinander stolpern, Menschen, die sich mit Maschinengewehren beschießen. Vor alledem: eine brennende Kinoleinwand mit einer Botschaft des Aufstands gegen Hitler und gegen den Faschismus ... Das Ereignis, das Tarantino hier inszeniert, hat es freilich nie gegeben. Gerade weil *Inglourious Basterds* sich nicht an geschichtliche Fakten hält, ist der Film sowohl interessant als auch problematisch. Wie ist das fiktive Attentat auf Hitler als filmischer Akt zu verstehen?

Ich möchte den Film hier vor allem durch zwei Perspektiven einführen. Erstens durch eine transatlantische Perspektive: Wie kann der Film aus amerikanischer und wie aus deutscher Sicht interpretiert werden? Das transatlantische Thema bietet sich besonders im Kontext eines Ortes wie Fluentum an, das sich in einem Gebäude befindet, das von den Nationalsozialisten gebaut und ab 1945 vom US-Militär genutzt wurde. Das derzeitige amerikanische Konsulat liegt bis heute direkt nebenan. Darüber hinaus diente es auch als Drehort für *Inglourious Basterds*, der größtenteils nicht weit entfernt auf dem Studiogelände in Babelsberg entstanden ist. Die zweite Frage, die ich aufgreifen möchte, ist, inwiefern *Inglourious Basterds* als Film über Filme betrachtet werden kann. Es ist ein Film, der zu einem wesentlichen Anteil in einem Kino stattfindet, Kinobetreiber*innen und Filmschaffende in den Vordergrund stellt und der in seiner audio-visuellen Sprache eindeutige Bezüge zu filmhistorisch wiedererkennbaren Stilmitteln, Genres und Epochen macht.

Es fällt mir dennoch nicht leicht, diesen Text zu schreiben, da ich sowohl gegenüber dem Kult um Regisseur Quentin Tarantino als auch gegenüber dem Film *Inglourious Basterds* ambivalente Gefühle und Gedanken habe. Zum einen aufgrund der für Tarantino typischen, cartoonhaften Inszenierung exzessiver Gewalt, die im Fall von *Inglourious Basterds* ähnlich locker im Kontext des realen historischen Traumas des Holocaust erzählt wird, wie der Regisseur es zuvor in rein fiktiven Erzählkontexten getan hatte. Zum anderen ist der Film von einer kontrafaktischen Erzählung durchdrungen, die die Geschichte des Zweiten Weltkriegs maßgeblich *um*schreibt. So ist der Film um zwei Parallelerzählungen strukturiert, in denen es um Planungen für Attentate auf Hitler geht, die so nie stattfanden. Hinzu kommt das eklektische Vermischen diverser Filmgenres und Stilmittel aus sowohl Avantgarde- als auch Mainstream-Hollywood-Kino, das – so könnte man durchaus argumentieren – gerade eine starke politische Botschaft darstellt – nicht über den Holocaust selbst, sondern über die Geschichte seiner Inszenierung.

Als ich den Film als Studentin kurz nach seinem Erscheinen zum ersten Mal sah, war ich zwar von einigen Szenen, insbesondere der Anfangssequenz, in der die junge französische Jüdin Shosanna Dreyfus Zeugin der Ermor-

Installation views of the C-print series *Once Upon a Time in Enemy-Occupied France* (2023). From the exhibition *Trash The Musical* by Loretta Fahrenholz, 2023.

more nuance than I had initially thought. I still see the film's moral ambivalence (or, as some critics have alleged, its moral superficiality). But the clever intertwinement of the numerous narrative strands, the presentation of language(s) and dialogue (which sometimes function as more dangerous weapons than the knives, baseball bats, and guns otherwise employed), and above all the way in which the film seems to "think" *as a* film *with* film *about* film convey a somewhat different picture to me now. Nevertheless, it is not my intention to conclusively evaluate the film in terms of good or bad, morally "right or wrong" here. I find it much more interesting to explore these mixed feelings, which some readers will probably share.

Like the rest of Tarantino's filmography, *Inglourious Basterds* is undoubtedly a "meta-movie"—a movie that constantly reminds its viewers that they are not watching a historical document but fiction. It repeatedly places film itself in the foreground. It does so directly, by incorporating the film industry as a motif in its narrative world or by directly naming Nazi filmmakers, in particular Leni Riefenstahl. It also does so by using film-within-a-film and by having the finale take place in a movie theater. Film thus appears capable of immense destruction at the same time that it literally saves the world. And *Inglourious Basterds* ultimately accomplishes this indirectly, via a whole series of visual and musical homages to iconic films, characters, and genres from film history that have been influential for Tarantino. The opening sequence's "widescreen Technicolor look," for example, as well as many of the fight scenes, evoke memories of John Ford's Westerns and Sergio Leone's Italian Westerns. The latter impression is reinforced by the use of music from the soundtracks of Italian Westerns composed by Ennio Morricone. It is a double allusion—to the Western itself, the most American of all film genres, and to the European exploitation of said genre. Conversely, *Inglourious Basterds* could be seen as an American exploitation of a story that takes place on European soil in order to form a critical and satirical look at precisely this exploitation: the way in which the Holocaust is portrayed in American cultural history.

My changed attitude towards *Inglourious Basterds* may likely be connected to living in the US for many years between both viewings. Through conversations with people in the US, especially with students, I have gained a more complex understanding of the differences between the German and American cultures of remembrance, especially with regard to the Holocaust. My perspective used to be very strongly influenced by the German culture of remembrance and media. In Germany—at least for the last twenty to thirty years or so—memories of the Holocaust and the Second World War are quite prominently incorporated into everyday life, school education, the public media, and, last but not least, cities and public spaces. Germany has often been lauded internationally as a role model for coming to terms and dealing with historical guilt—even if German approaches to the Holocaust have also faced mounting criticism in recent years for remaining too fixated on the past and treating it as isolated from current conflicts and expressions of antisemitism.

dung ihrer gesamten Familie wird, stark beeindruckt und berührt. Doch die Art und Weise, wie Tarantino seine Story (die immer wieder zwischen Thriller und Comedy hin- und herspringt) in den Kontext des Zweiten Weltkriegs und des Holocaust eingliedert, der mir mehr Unterhaltungshintergrund als wirklich Hauptgegenstand zu sein schien, kam mir unmoralisch vor. Wenn ich den Film jetzt wieder ansehe, stelle ich einen differenzierteren Blick darauf fest. Die moralische Ambivalenz des Films (oder, wie manche Kritiker ihm vorhielten, die moralische Oberflächlichkeit) sehe ich immer noch. Doch die clevere Verstrickung der vielen Erzählstränge, die Darstellung von Sprache(n) und Dialogen, die als teils gefährlichere Waffen fungieren als die Messer, Baseballschläger und Pistolen, die sonst noch zum Einsatz kommen, und vor allem die Art und Weise, wie der Film *als* Film *mit* Film *über* Film „nachzudenken" scheint, vermitteln mir jetzt ein etwas anderes Bild. Dennoch ist es hier nicht mein Anliegen, den Film abschließend als gut oder schlecht, als moralisch richtig oder moralisch falsch zu bewerten. Viel interessanter finde ich es, diesen gemischten Gefühlen, die einige Leser*innen wahrscheinlich mit mir teilen, nachzugehen.

So wie Tarantinos Werk allgemein, ist auch *Inglourious Basterds* ein absoluter „Metafilm" – das heißt, ein Film, der seinem Publikum immer wieder in Erinnerung ruft, dass es kein dokumentarisches Zeugnis, sondern einen fiktiven Film sieht. Es ist ein Film, der immer wieder Film an sich in den Vordergrund stellt. Dies tut er ganz direkt, indem er die Filmindustrie motivisch in seine Erzählwelt einbaut oder indem er historische Filmemacher*innen aus der NS-Zeit, insbesondere Leni Riefenstahl, namentlich im Film erwähnen lässt. Dies tut er auch, indem er Film-im-Film einsetzt und schließlich das Finale in einem Kino stattfinden lässt, infolgedessen womöglich Film sowohl viel Zerstörung anrichten, als auch im wahrsten Sinne des Wortes die Welt retten wird. Und dies tut er schließlich indirekt durch eine ganze Reihe visueller und musikalischer Hommagen an ikonische und für Tarantino einflussreiche Filme, Filmfiguren und Genres aus der Filmgeschichte. Der Widescreen-Technicolor-Look der Anfangssequenz zum Beispiel, ebenso wie viele der Kampfszenen, wecken Erinnerungen an die Western-Filme von John Ford, sowie die Italo-Western von Sergio Leone. (letzterer Eindruck wird durch den Einsatz mehrerer Stücke des Italo-Western-Komponisten Ennio Morricone noch verstärkt. Es ist eine doppelte Anspielung – auf den Western an sich, das amerikanischste aller Filmgenres, und an die europäische Verwertung jenes Genres. Umgekehrt könnte man *Inglourious Basterds* als eine amerikanische Verwertung einer auf europäischem Boden geschehenen Geschichte verstehen, die sich kritisch-satirisch mit genau dieser amerikanischen Verwertung, also der Art und Weise, wie der Holocaust in der amerikanischen Kulturgeschichte dargestellt wird, auseinandersetzt.

Dass sich meine eigene Einstellung zu *Inglourious Basterds* über die Jahre geändert hat, hat wahrscheinlich auch damit zu tun, dass ich mittlerweile viele Jahre in den USA verbracht habe. Ich habe in vielen Gesprächen mit Amerikaner*innen, insbesondere auch mit US-amerikanischen Studierenden, eine komplexere Vorstellung davon

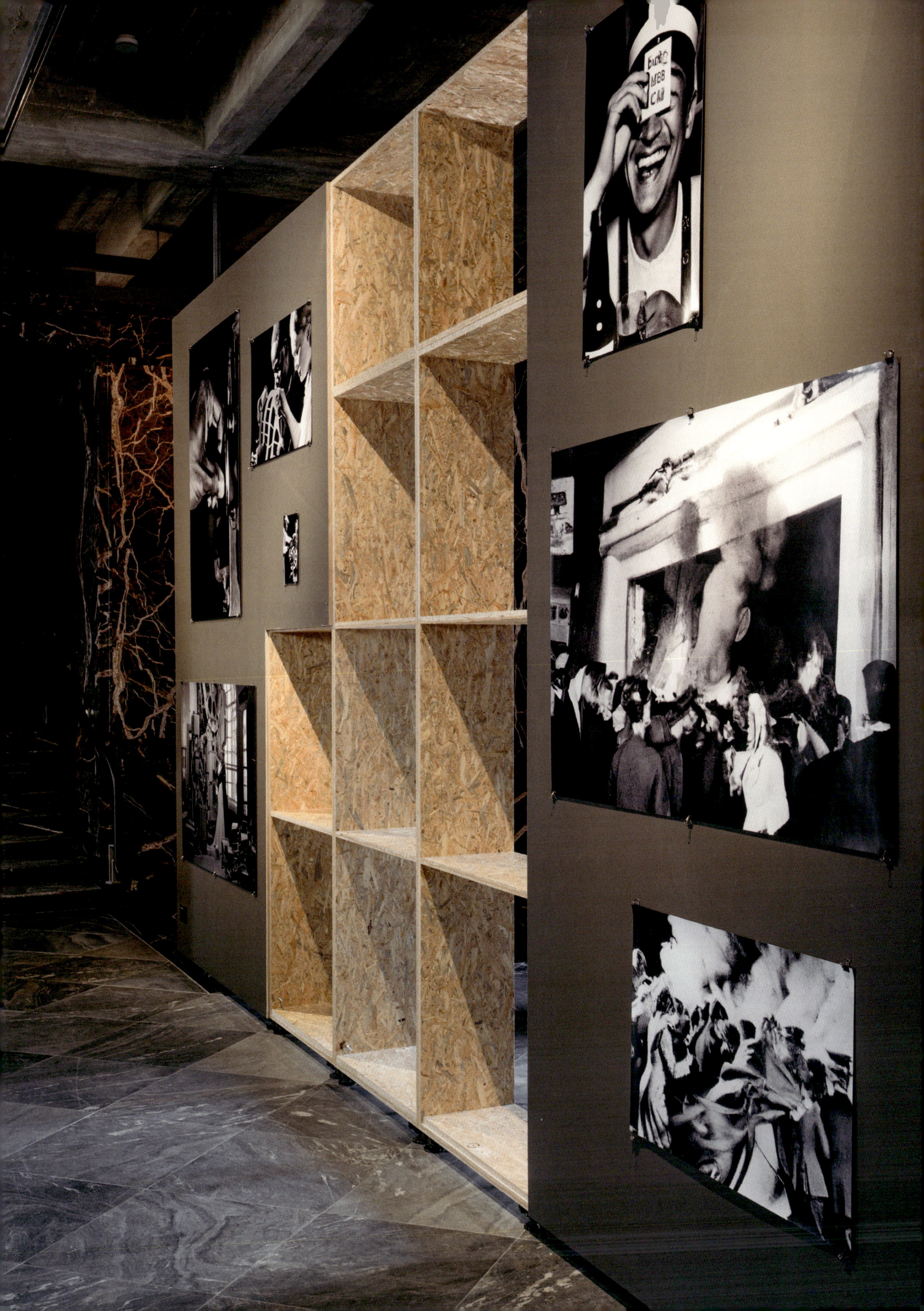

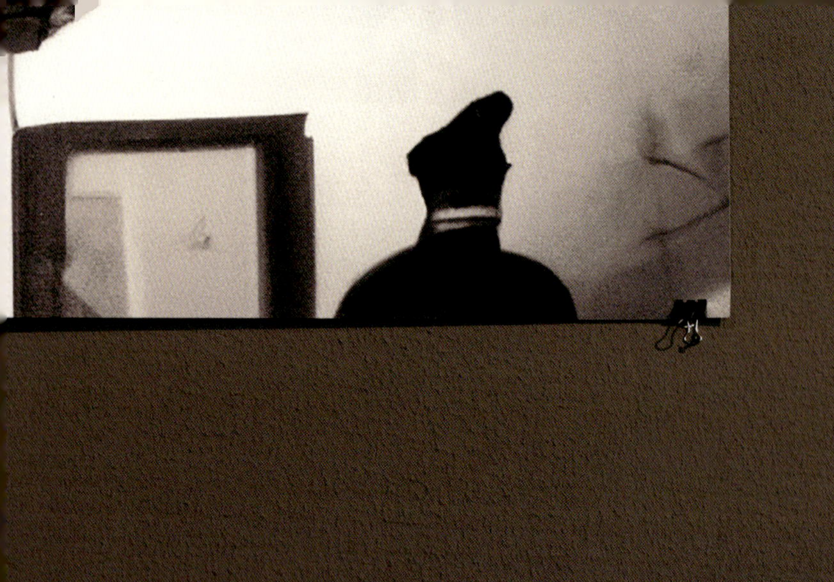

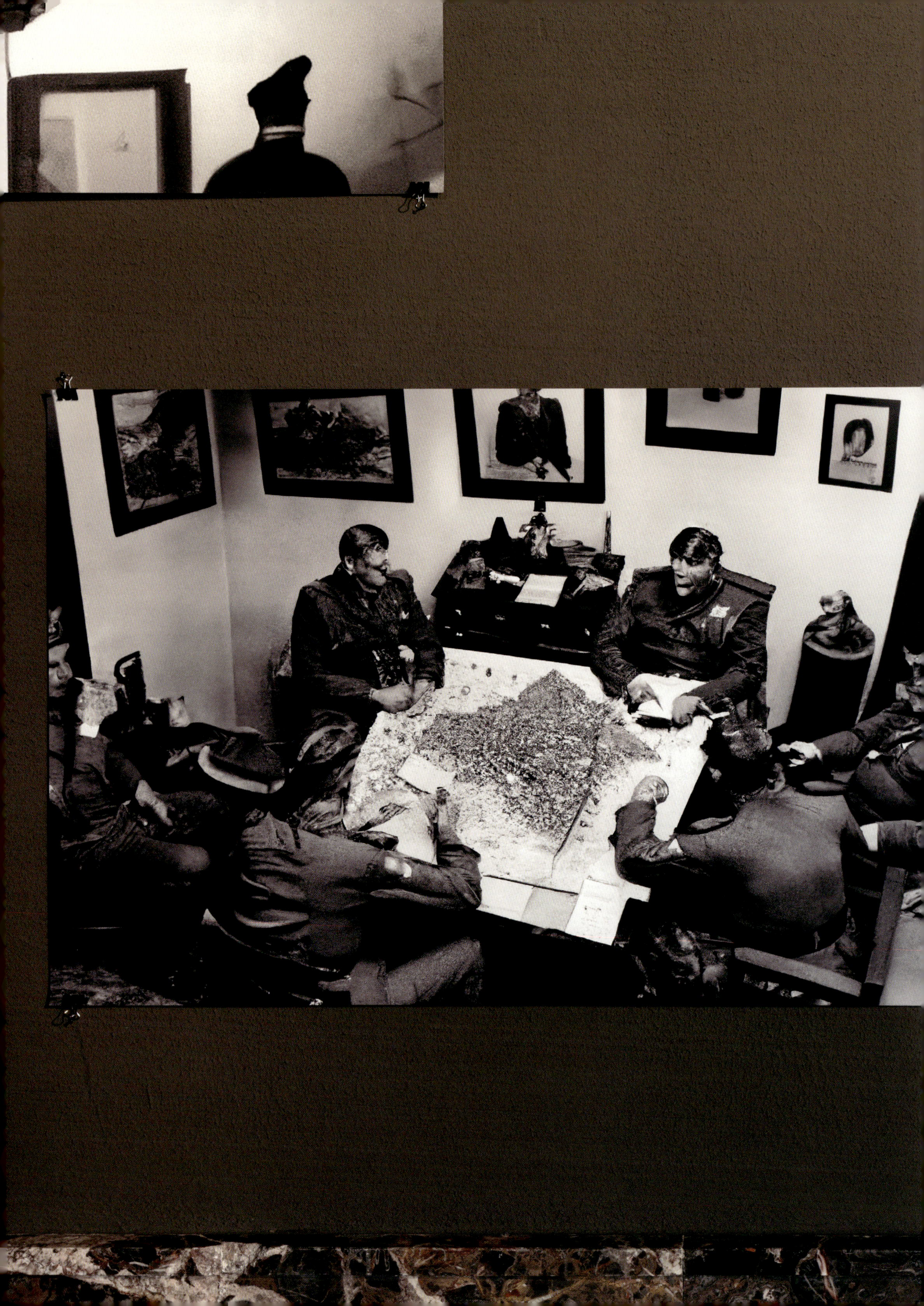

When I am out and about in Berlin with students from the United States, and we talk about the *Stolpersteine*[1] or the central location of the Memorial to the Murdered Jews of Europe, I usually hear positive, astonished reactions. In the United States, many places of remembrance are not as seamlessly integrated into city centers. In part, this has to do with the different spatial and traffic layouts of American cities. Yet, it also corresponds to a different culture of remembrance. In the case of Holocaust remembrance, however, its ubiquity within the German landscape is, of course, due to the fact that the Holocaust was perpetrated everywhere, in every city and on every street. Americans, especially younger generations, primarily know of the Holocaust through Hollywood films. When I ask American students what images first come to mind, it is not the photographs of piled-up glasses and suitcases, nor images of survivors and corpses from the liberated concentration camps, but the girl in the red coat from Steven Spielberg's film *Schindler's List* (1993) or the prison uniforms from Mark Herman's *The Boy in the Striped Pyjamas* (2008).

Literary scholar Stella Setka sees *Inglourious Basterds* as a critique of Hollywood's treatment of the Holocaust— of an American fascination with and exploitation of its history as mainstream entertainment, embedded within a strong heroic myth of American soldiers as the saviors of European Jews.[2] Tarantino indeed deviated from Hollywood conventions to some extent—among other things, by making the film radically multilingual instead of having it run entirely in English. But there are also grounds for challenging Setka's interpretation: Isn't he doing exactly what he is criticizing, according to Setka's reading? Namely, fictionalizing, Americanizing, and, ultimately, caricaturing the Holocaust?

This aspect was raised by several influential American critics who perceived the film as a trivialization of the Holocaust. David Denby wrote that it contained "counterfactual pop wish fulfillment and trashy exploitation."[3] Jonathan Rosenbaum even spoke of "Holocaust denial."[4] And both the American Daniel Mendelsohn[5] and the German Jens Jessen[6] accused Tarantino of prioritizing aesthetics over morality, of abusing Jewish fate for his cinematic bloodlust, and of turning the film's Jewish characters into versions of Nazis through their acts of violence. More favorable reviews usually, alongside praise for Christoph Waltz's acting, as well as his costars', emphasized the film's elements of fantasy—the fact that the film is avowedly *not* historically accurate and should not be misunderstood as such. Tarantino himself once stated that he wanted to create a narrative about genocide in general through his depiction of the Holocaust. In particular, he wanted to invite American audiences to reflect on the genocides in their own national history, including the genocide of the Americas' indigenous peoples.[7]

From the perspective of German Holocaust remembrance culture, such a generalizing tendency may be problematic, as Germany has been very careful in recent decades to uphold the unique historical position of the Holocaust. Jewish-American literary scholar Michael Rothberg, for example, was heavily criticized (and in my view politically misunderstood) by some in Germany for calling for

bekommen, welche Unterschiede es zwischen der deutschen und der amerikanischen Erinnerungskultur gibt, auch und gerade in Bezug auf den Holocaust. Meine Perspektive war früher sehr stark von der deutschen Erinnerungs- und Medienkultur geprägt. In Deutschland sind inzwischen – zumindest seit den letzten circa 20 bis 30 Jahren – Erinnerungen an den Holocaust und den Zweiten Weltkrieg recht prominent in das alltägliche Leben, in die Schulbildung, in die öffentlich-rechtlichen Medien und nicht zuletzt in Städte und öffentliche Räume integriert. Dafür ist Deutschland international oft als Vorbild für die Aufarbeitung und den Umgang mit der eigenen historischen Schuld hochgehalten worden – auch wenn der deutsche Umgang mit dem Holocaust in den letzten Jahren vermehrt dafür kritisiert wurde, diesen zu sehr in der Vergangenheit zu halten und von gegenwärtigen Konflikten und Ausdrücken von Antisemitismus zu trennen.

Wenn ich mit Studierenden aus Amerika in Berlin unterwegs bin und mit ihnen über die Stolpersteine oder den zentralen Standort des Denkmals für die ermordeten Juden Europas spreche, höre ich meist positive, erstaunte Reaktionen. In den USA sind solche Erinnerungsorte oftmals örtlich weiter ausgelagert und nicht auf dieselbe Weise in städtische Strukturen eingebettet, was teilweise mit den anderen Entfernungen und Verkehrssituationen zu tun haben mag, aber auch ein Hinweis auf eine andere Erinnerungskultur ist. Im Fall von Holocausterinnerung kommt die räumliche Integration bei uns jedoch natürlich auch entscheidend daher, dass der Holocaust hier überall, in jeder Stadt und jeder Straße, geschehen und verübt worden ist. In den USA dagegen kennen gerade jüngere Generationen den Holocaust insbesondere – oder sogar hauptsächlich – aus Hollywoodfilmen. Wenn ich US-Studierende frage, welche Bilder ihnen dazu als erstes in den Sinn kommen, dann sind es nicht die Fotografien der gestapelten Brillen und Koffer, auch nicht Aufnahmen der Überlebenden und der Leichen aus den befreiten Konzentrationslagern, sondern zunächst das Mädchen im roten Mantel aus Steven Spielbergs Film *Schindlers Liste* (1993) oder die Häftlingsuniformen aus Mark Hermans *Der Junge im gestreiften Pyjama* (2008).

Die Literaturwissenschaftlerin Stella Setka versteht daher *Inglourious Basterds* als Kritik an Hollywoods Verarbeitung des Holocaust: an einer amerikanischen Faszination für und die Ausbeutung von dessen Geschichte für Mainstream-Entertainment, die in einen starken Heldenmythos der amerikanischen Soldaten als Retter der europäischen Jüdinnen und Juden eingebettet ist.[1] Man kann diese Interpretation infrage stellen. Zwar weicht Tarantino teilweise von Hollywood-Konventionen ab – unter anderem dadurch, dass er den Film radikal mehrsprachig gestaltet, statt ihn komplett auf Englisch ablaufen zu lassen. Doch tut Tarantino dennoch nicht selbst genau das, was er, Setkas Lesart folgend, kritisiert? Nämlich eine Fiktionalisierung, Amerikanisierung, und letztlich eine Karikatur des Holocaust?

Interessanterweise war dies auch der Vorwurf mehrerer bedeutender amerikanischer Kritiker, die den Film als Trivialisierung des Holocaust auffassten. David Denby schrieb, der Film biete kontrafaktische, ausbeuterische Massenware [„counterfactual pop wish fulfillment and

Evelyn Kreutzer

Holocaust remembrance to be understood within a more global framework. Rothberg explained, "Remembrance always takes place in the present. By definition, it establishes a connection between the moment of remembering and the past. ... This fundamental property of memory means that the memory of the Holocaust, however singular it is historically, will necessarily ... be connected to other histories and to the present."[8] With these debates in mind, I would like to conclude with the following question: When we watch a film like *Inglourious Basterds*, or when we consume cultural entertainment about the Holocaust, to what extent are we dealing with a movie about the Holocaust and to what extent with a film about films (or entertainment about entertainment) about the Holocaust? And is this difference important?

Based on a lecture introducing a screening of *Inglourious Basterds* at Fluentum on July 28, 2023.

trashy exploitation"[2]. Jonathan Rosenbaum sprach sogar von „Holocaustleugnung" [„Holocaust denial"[3]. Und sowohl Daniel Mendelsohn auf amerikanischer[4] als auch Jens Jessen auf deutscher Seite[5] warfen Tarantino vor, Ästhetik über Moral zu stellen, das jüdische Schicksal für seine filmische Blutgier zu missbrauchen, und die jüdischen Figuren in dem Film durch ihre Gewalttaten selbst zu Kopien von Nazis zu machen. Positivere Kritiken stellten neben den schauspielerischen Leistungen von Christoph Waltz und seinen Kolleg*innen meist vor allem den Fantasy-Gedanken des Films heraus – also die Tatsache, dass der Film ganz explizit eben *nicht* historisch akkurat erzählt und somit auch nicht auf diese Weise missverstanden werden sollte. Tarantino selbst sagte einst, dass er durch seine Darstellung des Holocaust eine Erzählung über Genozid im Allgemeinen schaffen wollte. Er wollte vor allem das amerikanische Publikum dazu einladen, über die Genozide in ihrer eigenen Nationalgeschichte nachzudenken, unter anderem über den Genozid an der indigenen Bevölkerung Amerikas.[6]

Aus der deutschen Holocaust-Erinnerungskultur heraus mag dies problematisiert werden, da man in Deutschland in den letzten Jahrzehnten sehr darauf bedacht war, die historische Alleinstellung des Holocaust hochzuhalten. So wurde der amerikanisch-jüdische Literaturwissenschaftler Michael Rothberg in Deutschland teils stark dafür kritisiert (und in meinen Augen politisch missverstanden), dass er dazu aufrief, Holocausterinnerung stärker in einem globalen Zusammenhang zu verstehen. Rothberg erklärt: „Erinnerung findet immer in der Gegenwart statt. Definitionsgemäß stellt sie eine Verbindung zwischen dem Moment des Erinnerns und der Vergangenheit her [...]. Diese grundlegende Eigenschaft des Gedächtnisses bedeutet, dass die Erinnerung an den Holocaust, wie singulär er historisch auch ist, notwendigerweise [...] mit anderen Geschichten und mit der Gegenwart [...] in Verbindung stehen wird."[7] Abschließen möchte ich daher mit der folgenden Fragestellung: Wenn wir einen Film wie *Inglourious Basterds* schauen, beziehungsweise wenn wir Kultur- und Entertainmentprodukte mit Holocaust-Bezug konsumieren, inwiefern haben wir es mit einem Film über den Holocaust und inwiefern mit einem Film über Filme (beziehungsweise Entertainment über Entertainment) über den Holocaust zu tun? Und ist dieser Unterschied wichtig?

Basiert auf einem einführenden Vortrag anlässlich eines Screenings von *Inglourious Basterds* bei Fluentum am 28. Juli 2023.

1   Translator's note: *Stolpersteine*, literally "stumbling stones," are bronze plaques commemorating the victims of the Nazi regime in many German and European cities.
2   Stella Setka, "Bastardized History: How *Inglourious Basterds* Breaks through American Screen Memory," *Jewish Film & New Media* 3, no. 2 (2015), https://digitalcommons.wayne.edu/jewishfilm/vol3/iss2/.
3   David Denby, "Americans in Paris," *The New Yorker*, August 17, 2009, https://www.newyorker.com/magazine/2009/08/24/americans-in-paris.
4   Jonathan Rosenbaum, "Recommended Reading: Daniel Mendelsohn on the New Tarantino," Jonathan Rosenblaum, blog, July 29, 2019, https://jonathanrosenbaum.net/2019/07/recommended-reading-daniel-mendelsohn-on-the-new-tarantino/.
5   Daniel Mendelsohn, "Tarantino Rewrites the Holocaust," *Newsweek*, August 13, 2009, https://www.newsweek.com/tarantino-rewrites-holocaust-79003.
6   Jens Jessen, "Skalpiert die Deutschen!," *Die Zeit*, August 20, 2009, https://www.zeit.de/2009/35/Kino-Inglourious-Basterds?utm_referrer=https%3A%2F%2Fwww.google.com%2F.
7   Quentin Tarantino, "Quentin Tarantino: 'Inglourious' Child of Cinema," interview by Terry Gross, *NPR*, December 28, 2009, https://www.npr.org/transcripts/121969155.
8   Michael Rothberg, "Wir brauchen neue Wege, um über Erinnerung nachzudenken," interview by Elisabeth von Thadden, *Die Zeit*, March 27, 2021, https://www.zeit.de/kultur/2021-03/michael-rothberg-multidirektionale-erinnerung-buch-holocaust-rassismus-kolonialismus (translated by Lisa Contag).

1   Stella Setka, „Bastardized History: How Inglourious Basterds Breaks through American Screen Memory", in: *Jewish Film & New Media*, Jg. 3, Heft 2, Art. 2, 2015, https://digitalcommons.wayne.edu/jewishfilm/vol3/iss2/2 (letzter Zugriff: 06.10.2023).
2   David Denby, „Guts and Gloury", in: *The New Yorker*, 18.08.2009, https://www.newyorker.com/culture/richard-brody/guts-and-gloury (letzter Zugriff: 06.10.2023).
3   Jonathan Rosenbaum, „Recommended Reading: Daniel Mendelsohn on the New Tarantino", in: *jonathanrosenbaum.net*, 29.07.2019, https://jonathanrosenbaum.net/2019/07/recommended-reading-daniel-mendelsohn-on-the-new-tarantino/ (letzter Zugriff: 06.10.2023).
4   Daniel Mendelsohn, „Tarantino Rewrites the Holocaust", in: *Newsweek*, 13.08.2009, https://www.newsweek.com/tarantino-rewrites-holocaust-79003 (letzter Zugriff: 06.10.2023).
5   Jens Jessen, „Skalpiert die Deutschen!", in: *Die Zeit*, 20.08.2009, https://www.zeit.de/2009/35/Kino-Inglourious-Basterds?utm_referrer=https%3A%2F%2Fwww.google.com%2F (letzter Zugriff: 06.10.2023).
6   In einem Radio-Interview von Terry Gross: „Quentin Tarantino: ‚Inglourious' Child of Cinema", in: *NPR*, 27.08.2009. Transkript verfügbar unter https://www.npr.org/transcripts/121969155 (letzter Zugriff: 06.10.2023).
7   In einem Interview von Elisabeth von Thadden: „Wir brauchen neue Wege, um über Erinnerung nachzudenken", in: *Die Zeit*, 27.03.2021, https://www.zeit.de/kultur/2021-03/michael-rothberg-multidirektionale-erinnerung-buch-holocaust-rassismus-kolonialismus (letzter Zugriff: 06.10.2023).

Evelyn Kreutzer is a media scholar, video artist, and curator based in Lugano, Switzerland, and Berlin, Germany. She currently holds a postdoctoral position at Università della Svizzera italiana, as part of the SNSF-funded research group *The Video Essay: Memories, Ecologies, Bodies*. In both her written and practice-based work, she primarily focuses on exploring questions of memory, archival theory, and practice, as well as screen sound and music.

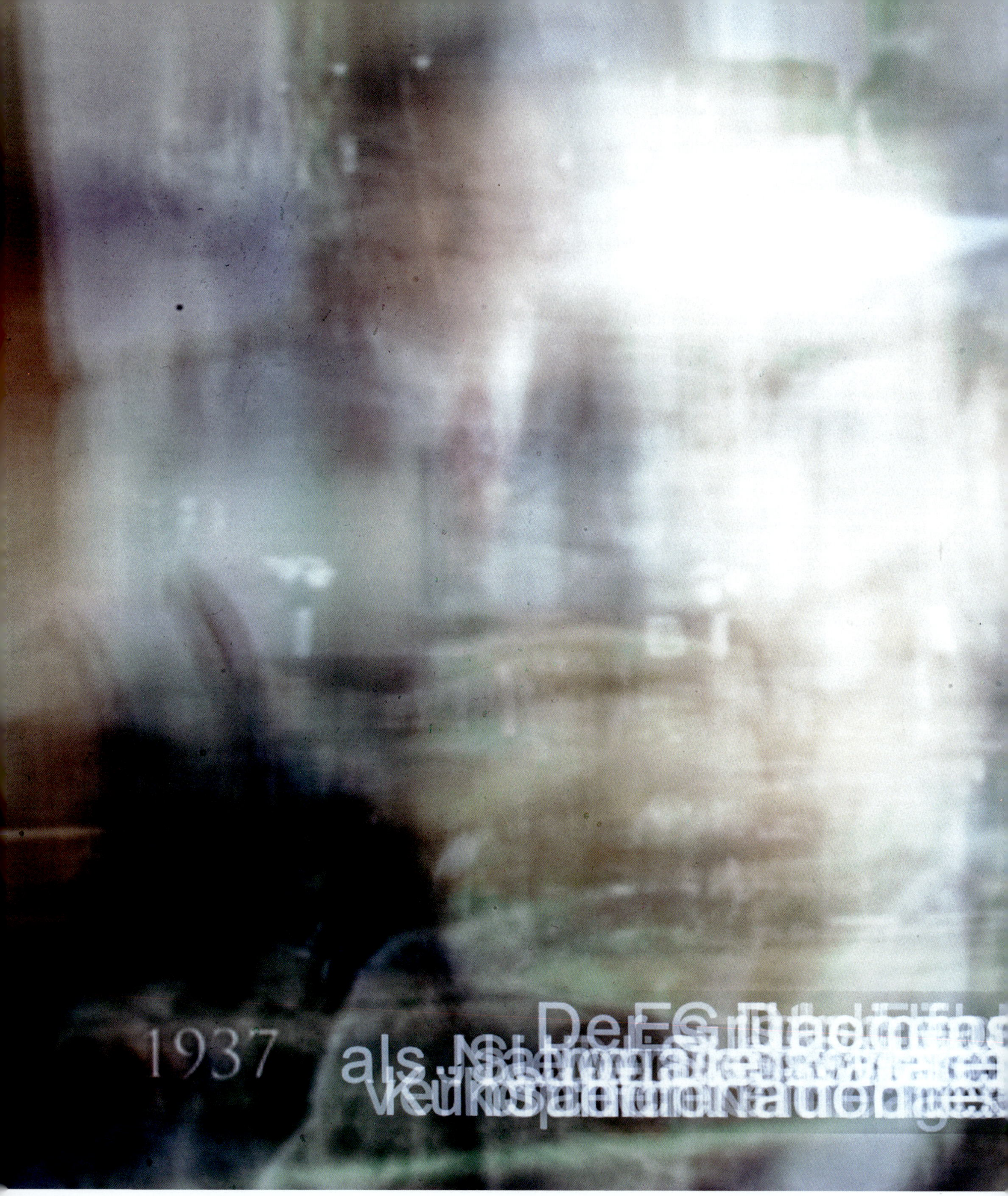

1937   als

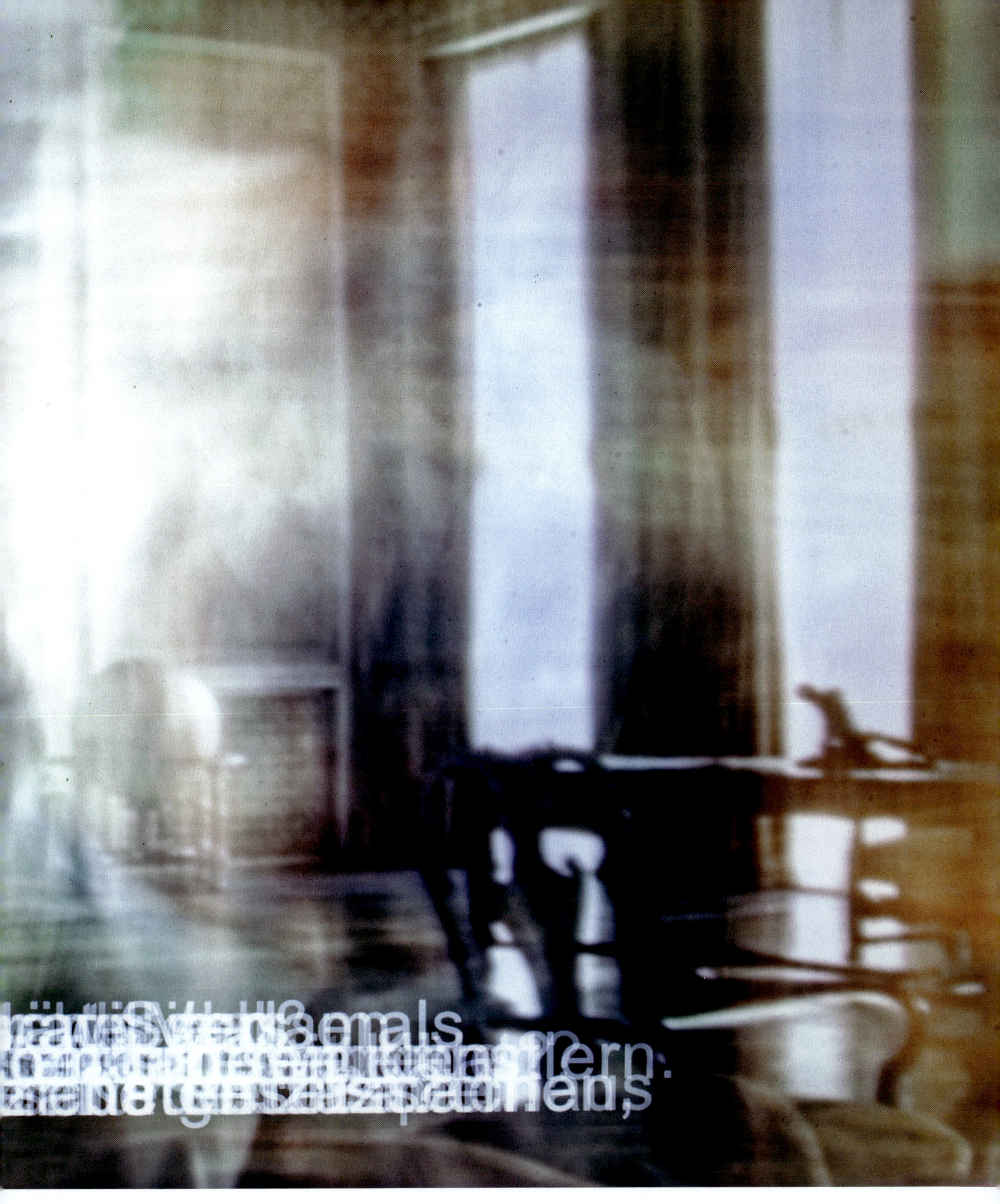

Maya Schweizer, *George Overlay*, 2024
Photographs nos. 1, 3, and 4 from a series of 6

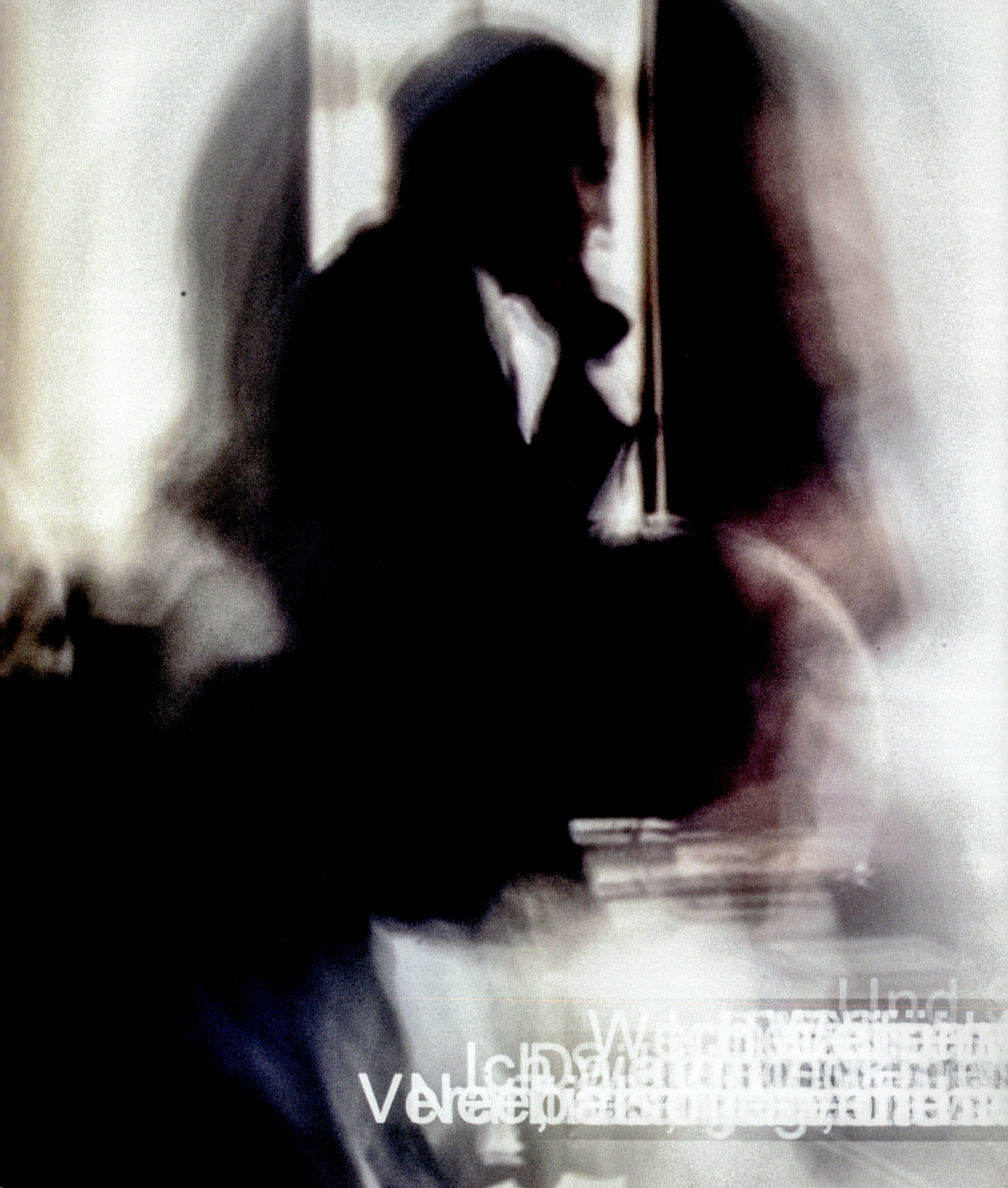

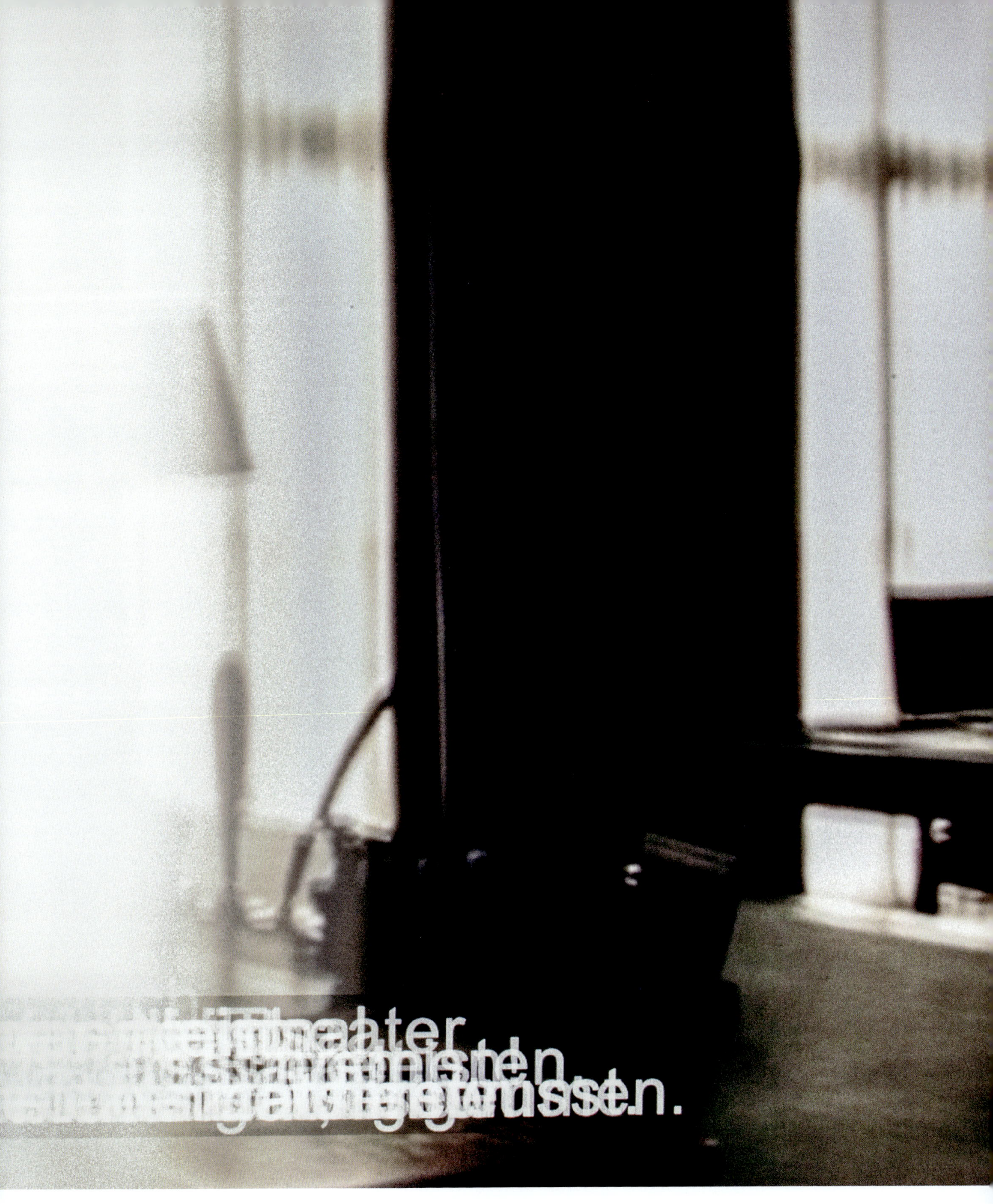

Maya Schweizer

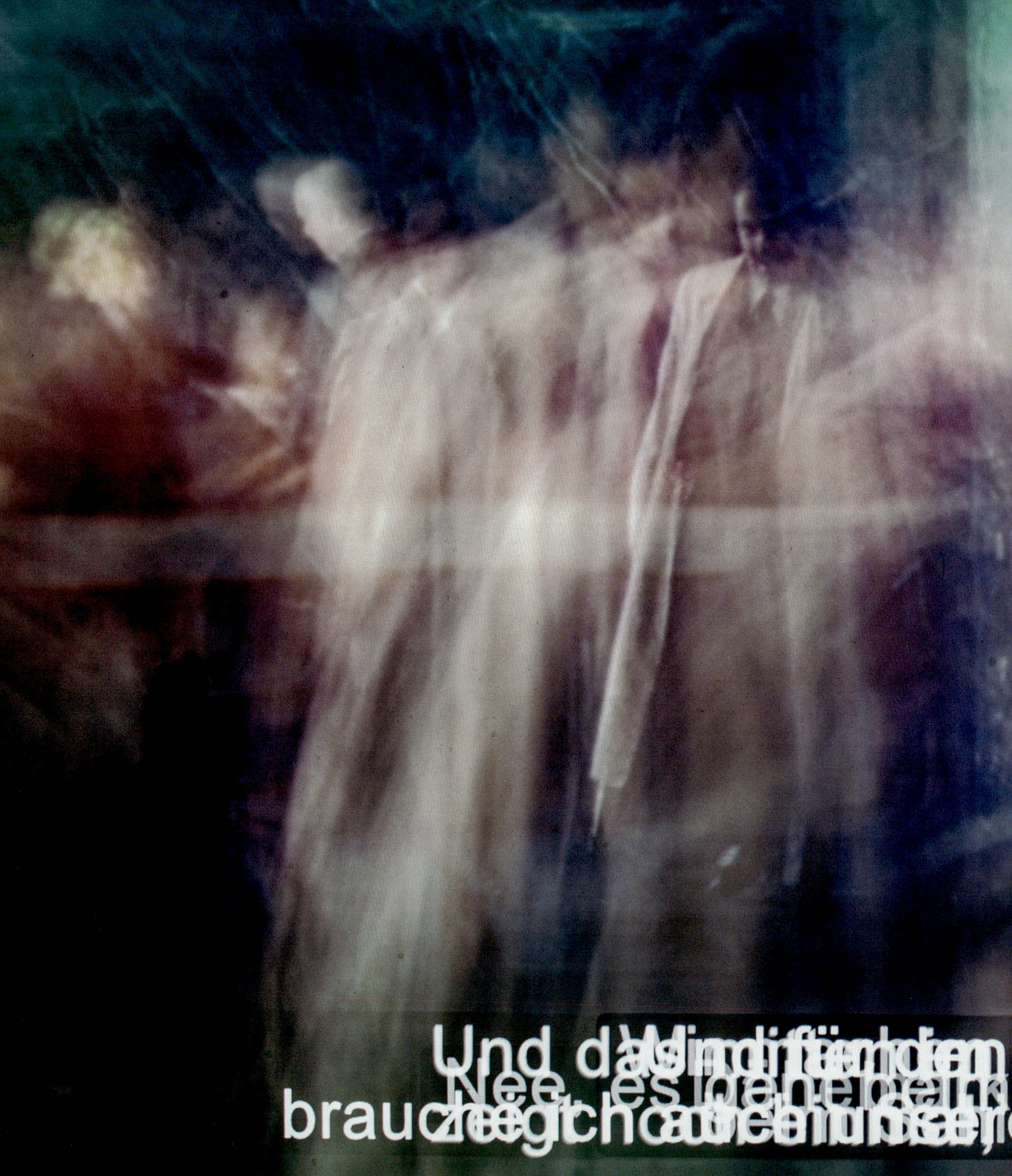

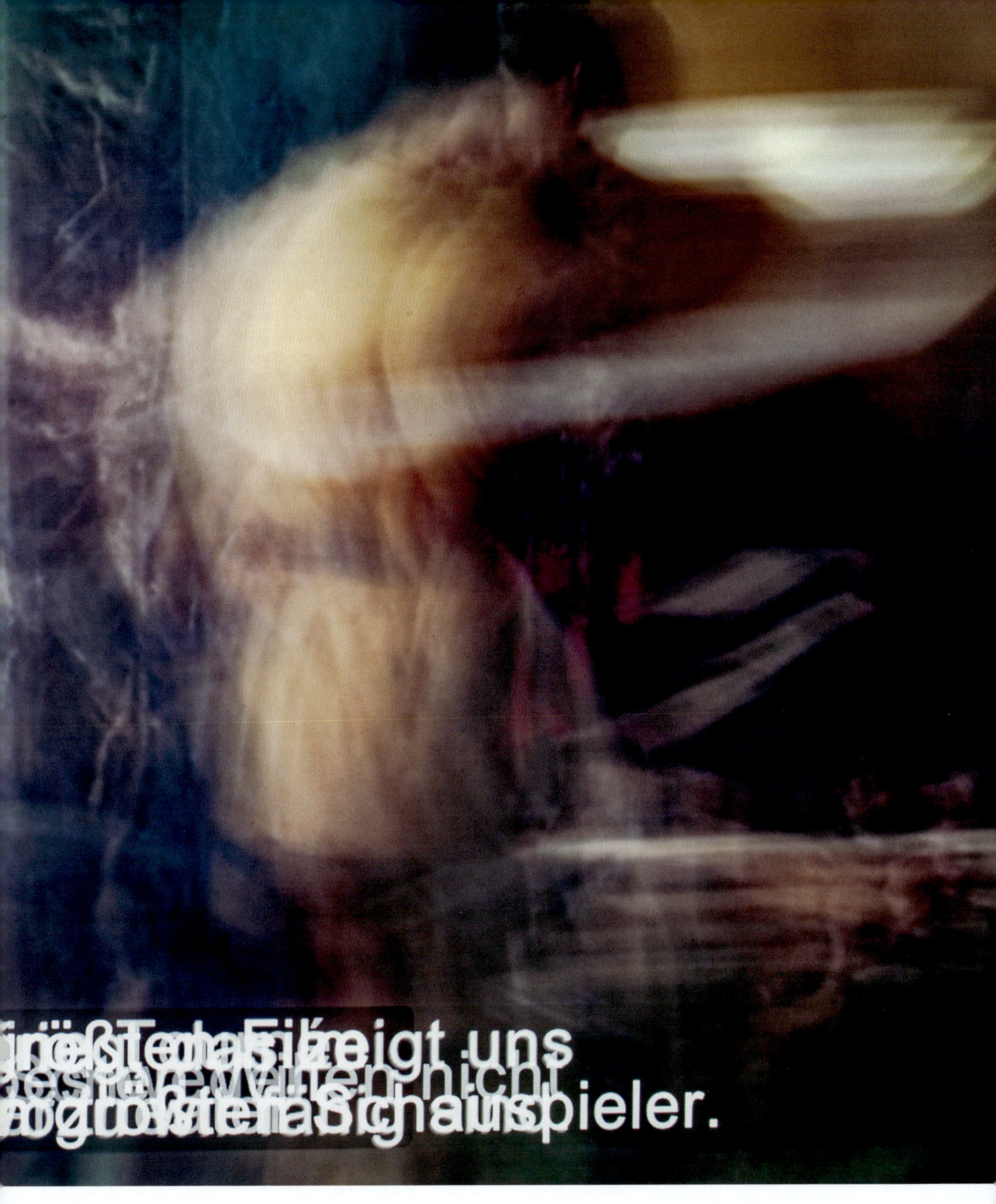

Maya Schweizer

Thomas Helbig
George and the (Hi)stories That Cinema Writes

> "Let social conditions be what they will, if only he can carry on, a decent peddler."[1]

The German television film *George* (directed by Joachim A. Lang; 2013) attempted a search for historical and biographical traces of Heinrich George (1893–1946), whose work as an exceptionally talented actor in theater and film made him one of the most popular figures in Germany in the first half of the twentieth century. The medium in this biographical approach is his son Götz George (1938–2016), who later followed in his father's footsteps. This legacy is the film's hidden leitmotif, whose problematic nature is already hinted at by the ambiguous title: Which George does it refer to?

On the one hand, the film contains documentary material, such as film clips, photographs, and audio recordings, paired with excerpts from feature films starring Heinrich George in his major roles. On the other hand, the film includes staged segments in which Götz George performs scenes from his father's life—between film and family life—as cinematic reenactments. The glue for this mixture, which remains speculative for long stretches, consists of historical locations and a soft-focus vintage aesthetic, but also costumes that, as in a uniform worn by Martin Wuttke when he slips into the role of Goebbels, often don't quite fit. The overwrought acting and the constant switching between documentary and fiction create a crude mélange that suggests both forceful and unconditional evidentiary power. This is accomplished not least by the scenes featuring contemporaries of Heinrich recounting their memories alongside Götz George and his brother Jan George.

Beyond the factuality of the testimonies and documents, it is above all the film's form that enforces a uniform emphasis, which becomes immediately apparent from the film's opening. Documentary footage of a destroyed Berlin in December 1945 merges seamlessly into a "reverse shot" of the supposed beholder of this gaze. It is George's wife, Berta Drews, looking out of the window of a Berlin tram with her son Götz (played by Muriel Baumeister and Luis Kain). The shot ends with a close-up of the child's face, while Götz George's off-screen voice segues into Heinrich George's production of Goethe's *Faust*, which he rehearsed with prisoners while in Soviet captivity. This is followed by a close-up of the real Götz George's face, who, immersed in the warm lighting of the sparse stage, is playing his father. Even the mere description of this complicated constellation illustrates the extent of the historical gaps being bridged here through filmic means. This finally culminates in a dramatic scene of the father's reunion with his child, i.e., the fictional alter ego meeting his grown-up double, who is in turn embodying his deceased father. This "prelude"[2] is the film's *La Jetée* moment: the son spies the figure of his father through the fog of the Hohenschönhausen prison camp and runs past the guards through the gate, which opens by chance, straight into his father's arms. This final embrace between father and child—young Götz was only seven years old at the time—is etched into the child's memory, and has since

Thomas Helbig
George und die Geschichte(n), die das Kino schreibt

> „Die gesellschaftlichen Bedingungen dürfen sein, wie sie wollen, wenn er, der ehrliche Hausierer, nur weitermachen kann."[1]

Die deutsche Fernsehproduktion *George* (Joachim A. Lang, 2013) versucht sich an einer historisch-biografischen Spurensuche, die dem Ausnahmetalent Heinrich George (1893–1946) gewidmet ist, der als Schauspieler für Theater und Film zu einer der populärsten Figuren in der ersten Hälfte des 20. Jahrhunderts avancierte. Das Medium dieser biografischen Annäherung ist dessen Sohn Götz George (1938–2016), der dem Beruf seines Vaters folgte. Das Erbe dieses Schattens ist das heimliche Leitmotiv des Films, dessen Problematik sich bereits in der Indifferenz des Titels andeutet. Welcher „George" ist hier gemeint?

Gegenstand des Films sind einerseits dokumentarische Aufnahmen, das heißt Film-, Foto- und Tondokumente, gepaart mit Ausschnitten aus Spielfilmen, in denen Heinrich George seine großen Rollen hatte. Andererseits enthält die Produktion Spielfilm-Anteile, in denen Götz George Szenen aus dem Leben des Vaters – zwischen Kino- und Familienleben – als filmische Reenactments aufführt. Als Kitt dieser über weite Strecken spekulativ bleibenden Mischung halten historische Schauplätze, ein weichzeichnender Vintage-Look, aber auch Kostümierungen her, die, wie im Falle der Uniform Martin Wuttkes, der in die Rolle von Goebbels schlüpft, oft nicht so recht passen wollen. Das distanzlose Spiel und der ständige Wechsel zwischen dokumentarischen und fiktionalen Elementen erzeugen eine krude Melange, die eine so eindringliche wie unbedingte Beweiskraft suggerieren. Dafür sollen nicht zuletzt jene Szenen sorgen, in denen neben Götz George und dessen Bruder Jan George weitere Zeitzeugen zu Wort kommen, die aus ihren Erinnerungen berichten.

Es ist vor allem die Form des Films, die, über die Faktizität der Zeugnisse und Dokumente hinaus, den Konformismus der Emphase erzwingt, was sich bereits zu Beginn des Films unmittelbar aufdrängt. Dokumentarische Aufnahmen des zerstörten Berlins vom Dezember 1945 gehen bruchlos über in einen Gegenschuss auf das vermeintliche Subjekt dieses Blickes. Es ist die Ehefrau Georges, Berta Drews, die zusammen mit ihrem Sohn Götz, gespielt von Muriel Baumeister und Luis Kain, aus dem Fenster einer Berliner Stadtbahn blickt. Die Einstellung endet mit einem Close-up auf das Gesicht des Kindes, während die Stimme Götz Georges aus dem Off einsetzend auf Heinrich Georges Inszenierung von Goethes *Faust* überleitet, die dieser in sowjetischer Gefangenschaft gemeinsam mit Häftlingen einstudiert hat. Dann ein Close-up auf das Gesicht des echten Götz Georges, der, in das warme Licht der kargen Bühne getaucht, seinen Vater mimt. Schon bei der bloßen Beschreibung dieser vertrackten Konstellation wird deutlich, welche historischen Klüfte hier filmisch überbrückt werden. Dies gipfelt schließlich in der dramatischen Szene der Begegnung des Vaters mit seinem Kind, das heißt des fiktiven Alter Egos, das auf sein erwachsen gewordenes Doppel trifft, das seinerseits den verstorbenen Vater verkör-

been verified by witnesses several times along roughly the same lines.[3] George died in the Sachsenhausen Special Camp in 1946.

Living with this memory and the loss it represents would have been enough material for a film, but this one obviously has something else in mind. George's role as a husband, family man, friend, and theater director becomes the pivotal point of a cinematic investigation, whose conclusion will undertake something like a political exoneration of Heinrich George, likely the most prominent state actor of the Third Reich.[4]

After George had performed on stage with Erwin Piscator and Bertolt Brecht and received important roles in Weimar Republic cinema in Fritz Lang's *Metropolis* (1927), as Émile Zola in *Dreyfus* (Richard Oswald; 1930), and as Franz Biberkopf in *Berlin Alexanderplatz* (Phil Jutzi; 1931), his appearance in Hans Steinhoff's *Our Flag Leads Us Forward* (*Hitlerjunge Quex;* 1933) definitively signaled a political shift, which would continue in his subsequent engagements. *George* references the haunting scene in which George, playing a worker and Communist, brutally and crudely forces his son to sing "The Internationale." It is a film about the infectious fascination that emanated from National Socialism, which makes the father's Communist views seem like relics from a bygone era in comparison. The boy experiences a momentous conflict of loyalties. Quex increasingly finds himself caught between two sides: one the one hand, his sense of duty towards his father, and on the other, his allegiance to his fellow Hitler Youth members. He decides against his father and the latter's comrades, with the film presenting the betrayal of the Communists as a worthy cause that ultimately requires the boy's martyrdom. From today's perspective, the film is especially remarkable for portraying this political conversion as less a question of political conviction than a matter of common sense.[5] In light of *George*'s father-son entanglement, the loss of the son (Berta Drews plays the mother) stands out in *Our Flag Leads Us Forward*, with Quex experiencing his initiation as a "*Hitlerjunge*" as a liberation from familial dependence and subordination. This is only rendered plausible by the father's blind brutality ("My boy a Nazi? ... I'd rather beat him to death.") and the "caricature of the Communist opponent."[6] As depicted in *George*, Götz George's own relationship with his father contains no sign of such conflicts of loyalty. And herein lies this film's blind spot, which consistently tries to ignore George's responsibility for the consequences of his screen presence. For example, there is no discussion of the fact that George acted in *Jew Süß* (*Jud Süß*; 1940),[7] a film directed by Veit Harlan to serve as antisemitic Nazi propaganda. It has been well-documented that SS units, camp guards, and police officers in particular were obliged to watch the film.[8]

The staged conversation between Goebbels and George about working on Harlan's *Kolberg* (1945), which the minister of propaganda had commissioned to be a last stand of "intellectual warfare," is probably the most daring setting in *George*.[9] The scene presents George, fearing sanctions against the Berlin Schiller Theater (which he directed), as being virtually forced into participating in the film. There are no records of the actual conversation. As a

pert. Dieses „Vorspiel"[2] ist das *La Jetée*-Moment des Films: Der Sohn entdeckt durch den Nebel des Häftlingslagers in Hohenschönhausen die Gestalt des Vaters und rennt, durch das zufällig aufgehende Tor, an den Wachposten vorbei, direkt in die Arme des Vaters. Diese letzte Umarmung zwischen Vater und Kind – der kleine Götz ist gerade einmal sieben Jahre alt – hat sich in das Gedächtnis des Kindes eingebrannt und sie wird später, so oder so ähnlich, noch mehrfach bezeugt.[3] 1946 stirbt George im Speziallager Sachsenhausen.

Das Leben mit dieser Erinnerung und dem Verlust, den sie bedeutet, wäre schon Film genug gewesen, doch dieser hat offenbar etwas anderes im Sinn. Georges Rolle als Ehemann, Familienvater, Freund und Theaterintendant wird zum Dreh- und Angelpunkt einer filmischen Recherche, an deren Ende so etwas wie die politische Entlastung Heinrich Georges, des wohl prominentesten Staatsschauspielers des Dritten Reichs, stehen soll.[4]

Nachdem George bei Erwin Piscator und Bertolt Brecht am Theater spielte und mit Fritz Langs *Metropolis* (1927), als Émile Zola in *Dreyfus* (Richard Oswald, 1930) oder als Franz Biberkopf in *Berlin Alexanderplatz* (Phil Jutzi, 1931) bedeutende Rollen im Kino der Weimarer Republik erhielt, deutet spätestens sein Auftritt in Hans Steinhoffs *Hitlerjunge Quex* (1933) auf Anzeichen eines politischen Vorzeichenwechsels, der sich auch in seinen nachfolgenden Engagements fortsetzte. *George* zitiert daraus die eindringliche Szene, in der George, der einen Arbeiter und Kommunisten spielt, seinen Sohn auf brutale und grobschlächtige Weise dazu zwingt, die Internationale zu singen. Es ist ein Film über die ansteckende Faszination, die vom Nationalsozialismus ausging, neben dem die kommunistische Gesinnung des Vaters wie ein Relikt aus vergangenen Zeiten anmutet. Der Junge durchlebt einen folgenreichen Loyalitätskonflikt. Das Pflichtgefühl gegenüber dem Vater auf der einen und die Verbundenheit mit den Kameraden der Hitlerjugend auf der anderen Seite, gerät Quex zunehmend zwischen die Fronten. Er entscheidet sich gegen den Vater und dessen Kameraden, wobei der Film den Verrat an den Kommunisten als gerechte Sache inszeniert, die schließlich den (Märtyrer-)Tod des Jungen erfordert. Aus heutiger Sicht bemerkenswert ist die Tatsache, dass der Film den politischen Vorzeichenwechsel weniger als Frage politischer Gesinnung, denn als Gebot der Vernunft darstellt.[5] Mit Blick auf die Vater-Sohn-Verschränkung von *George* sticht in *Hitlerjunge Quex* insbesondere die Lossagung des Sohnes – Berta Drews spielt die Mutter – hervor, der mit seiner Initiation zum Hitlerjungen die Befreiung von familiärer Fremdbestimmung und Unmündigkeit erlebt. Glaubwürdig wird dies nur durch die blindwütige Brutalität des Vaters („Mein Junge und Nazi? [...] Eher schlag' ich ihn tot.") und die „Karikatur des kommunistischen Gegners".[6] In der Beziehung von Götz George zu seinem Vater, wie er in *George* dargestellt wird, ist von solchen Loyalitätskonflikten freilich nichts zu spüren. Und hier liegt der blinde Fleck dieses Films, der permanent von Georges Verantwortung für die Funktion und Effekte seiner Leinwandpräsenz abzusehen versucht. So fehlt etwa die Auseinandersetzung damit, dass George 1939 als Schauspieler für den Film *Jud Süß* (1940) engagiert wurde.[7] Ein Film, der unter der Regie von Veit Harlan gezielt

historical artifact, *Kolberg* speaks for itself: George plays the upright mayor Nettelbeck, who mobilizes his people to stand up to Napoleon's troops alongside the military, led by Major von Gneisenau. Goebbels, who identified with the character and personally contributed to the screenplay, wanted to use *Kolberg* to stage the people's willing "sacrifice" (the title of Harlan's previous film). The premiere on January 30, 1945, accordingly took place not only in the "ruined city of Berlin," but also in the embattled Atlantic fortress of La Rochelle, where a copy of the film was dropped by parachute.[10] The fact that the fortress of La Rochelle surrendered shortly after, and that "Kolberg fell into Soviet hands while the film *Kolberg* was running," was irrelevant.[11] The "storm" conjured up in the film's finale was nothing more than cinematic fiction.

Siegfried Kracauer characterized Heinrich George as an "honest peddler" with a "tumbler attitude" who overcomes all circumstances in his role of Franz Biberkopf. Perhaps he was also making a statement about George the man, and all the more so if Kracauer's following assertion were also true: "He is not the one playing the role, he adapts the role to himself. George is not Biberkopf; rather, the latter takes on George's traits."[12]

George stages the dialogue between the propaganda minister and the state actor in a location steeped in history, which has often served as a film set. The scene was filmed in the "dining room" of the former Luftgaukommando III in Berlin's Dahlem neighborhood, which today houses Fluentum's exhibition space. While it's fiction that the propaganda minister lived there, it is true that the buildings were used as the US headquarters at the end of the war, and may even have been frequented by presidents. For the film *George*, the traces of these changes of function were temporarily erased in favor of creating a (seemingly) coherent sense of a specific place and time. To the left and right of the window, bellicose quotes from Franklin D. Roosevelt and John F. Kennedy can still be found today. But they are the sediments of other (hi)stories.

"We, too, born to freedom, and believing in freedom, are willing to fight to maintain freedom. We, and all others who believe as we do, would rather die on our feet than live on our knees." (Roosevelt)

"The world must know that we will fight for Berlin. We will never permit that city to fall under Communist influence. We are defending the freedom of Paris and New York when we stand up for freedom in Berlin." (Kennedy)

Thomas Helbig is an art historian based in Frankfurt am Main. He studied Fine Arts, Art History, and Philosophy in Dresden and Berlin. He received his PhD from Humboldt University in Berlin for his work on Jean-Luc Godard's video essay *Histoire(s) du cinéma*. The dissertation was awarded the 2021 Rudolf Arnheim Prize. He is currently a Research Associate at the Institute of Art History at Goethe University in Frankfurt.

zur antisemitischen Propaganda des Nationalsozialismus eingesetzt wurde. Es ist vielfach überliefert, dass insbesondere SS-Einheiten, Lager-Wachmannschaften und Polizisten dazu verpflichtet wurden, den Film zu sehen.[8]

Das inszenierte Gespräch zwischen Goebbels und George, in dem es um die Mitarbeit an Harlans monumentalem Durchhaltefilm *Kolberg* (1945) geht, den der Propagandaminister als letztes Aufgebot „geistiger Kriegsführung" in Auftrag gab, ist die wahrscheinlich gewagteste Setzung in *George*.[9] Demnach scheint George, der Sanktionen gegen das von ihm geleitete Berliner Schillertheater fürchtete, die Mitwirkung an dem Film förmlich abgerungen worden zu sein. Wie das Gespräch tatsächlich verlief, ist schlicht nicht nachweisbar. Den Film in den Zeugenstand der Geschichte gerufen, spricht *Kolberg* für sich: George spielt darin den aufrechten Bürgermeister Nettelbeck, der seine Bevölkerung mobilisiert, um sich gemeinsam mit dem Militär, geführt von Gneisenau, gegen die Truppen Napoleons zu stellen. Goebbels, der sich mit dieser Figur identifizierte und selbst am Drehbuch mitwirkte, wollte mit *Kolberg* den bereitwilligen „Opfergang" (so der Titel von Harlans vorigem Film) des Volkes inszenieren. Die Premiere am 30. Januar 1945 fand deshalb nicht nur in der „Ruinenstadt Berlin" statt, sondern auch in der umkämpften Atlantikfestung La Rochelle, wo eine Kopie des Films per Fallschirmabwurf abgesetzt wurde.[10] Dass sich die Festung La Rochelle kurze Zeit darauf ergab und dass „Kolberg in sowjetische Hand fiel, während der Film *Kolberg* lief", durfte keine Rolle spielen.[11] Der „Sturm", der im Finale des Films heraufbeschworen wurde, war nichts weiter als filmische Fiktion.

Siegfried Kracauer charakterisierte Heinrich George in seiner Rolle des Franz Biberkopf einst als „ehrlichen Hausierer" mit einer über alle Verhältnisse erhabenen „Stehaufmännchenhaltung". Möglicherweise hat er damit auch etwas über den Menschen „George" ausgesagt und dies um so mehr, wenn auch die folgende Behauptung Kracauers zuträfe: „Er ist nicht Träger der Rolle, er paßt die Rolle sich an. Nicht George ist Biberkopf; der nimmt die Züge Georges an."[12]

Den Dialog zwischen dem Propagandaminister und dem Staatsschauspieler verortet *George* an einem geschichtsträchtigen Ort, der bereits häufiger als Filmkulisse diente. Die Szene wurde im „Speisesaal" des ehemaligen Luftgaukommando III in Berlin-Dahlem gedreht, in dem sich heute die Ausstellungsräume von Fluentum befinden. Es ist eine Fiktion, dass der Propagandaminister dort seine Räume gehabt hätte, wahr ist jedoch, dass die Gebäude mit Kriegsende als US-Hauptquartier genutzt wurden, in denen möglicherweise sogar Präsidenten ein- und ausgingen. Für den Film *George* wurden die Spuren dieser Umnutzung zugunsten einer (scheinbar) kohärenten Orts- und Zeitspezifik vorübergehend getilgt. Links und rechts auf der Fensterseite finden sich auch heute noch die kämpferischen Zitate von Franklin D. Roosevelt und John F. Kennedy. Doch dies sind die Sedimente anderer (Ge-)Schichten.

„We, too, born to freedom, and believing in freedom, are willing to fight to maintain freedom. We, and all others who believe as we do, would rather die on our feet than live on our knees." (Roosevelt)

„The world must know that we will fight for Berlin. We will never permit that city to fall under Communist influence. We are defending the freedom of Paris and New York when we stand up for freedom in Berlin." (Kennedy)

1   Siegfried Kracauer, *From Caligari to Hitler* (Princeton, NJ: Princeton University Press, 2019), 359.
2   The recitation is from "Vorspiel auf dem Theater," the first scene in Goethe's *Faust*.
3   Berta Drews, actress and wife of Heinrich George, described this meeting in her memoirs. Berta Drews, *Heinrich George. Ein Schauspielerleben* (Hamburg: Rowohlt, 1959), 11 et seq. See also Joachim A. Lang, *Heinrich George. Eine Spurensuche* (Leipzig: Flügel & Sohn GmbH, 2013), 16.
4   In this respect, the film is similar to the earlier television film *Wenn sie mich nur spielen lassen* (directed by Irmgard von zu Mühlen; 1997), which was produced shortly after George was rehabilitated by Russia. In it, Götz George states, "I think that after fifty years there should be no more criticism. ... We should now slowly begin the hour of celebration." Cf. also Lang, *Heinrich George*, 154.
5   In a close reading of the scene, Erwin Leiser concludes with Gregory Bateson "that the characterization of the Communists in this film is a self-portrait of the National Socialists. ... The 'ham knocking,' by which the Communists ... are characterized as a brutal and undisciplined horde, was in fact often played by the Hitler Youth. The Communists are portrayed as the antithesis of National Socialist ideals, whereby the attributes assigned to the Communists have their psychological roots in the character of the National Socialists." Erwin Leiser, *"Deutschland erwache!" Propaganda im Film des Dritten Reiches*, expanded new edition (Hamburg: Rowohlt, 1978), 41 (translated by Lisa Contag). See also Leiser's film *Deutschland erwache: Film als Propaganda des NS-Staates* (1967/68). Rüdiger Suchsland's film *Hitlers Hollywood. Das deutsche Kino im Zeitalter der Propaganda 1933–1945* (2016/17) also deals with this scene.
6   Leiser, *"Deutschland erwache!"*, 37 (translated by Lisa Contag).
7   This brings to mind another famous father-son relationship: Thomas Harlan spent his life grappling with the role and function that his father's films played for the Nazis. This is where he identifies his father's real guilt and failure, resulting from films such as *Jew Süß*: "If you have made a hammer others [were] beaten to death with, you can no longer be a hammer maker. ... Can you still be a director?" With resoluteness, he wrestled with his father's legacy, impressively documented in the feature-length film discussion *Wandersplitter* (Christoph Hübner and Gabriele Voss; 2004–06).
8   Leiser, *"Deutschland erwache!"*, 79.
9   Harlan was not only granted complete financial freedom for his film ("The film could cost whatever was needed." Quote from Thomas Harlan, *Veit* (Hamburg: Rowohlt, 2011), 122), he was also given the grotesquely high number of 187,000 soldiers for the (later shortened) battle scenes (according to his own statements). Leiser *"Deutschland erwache!"*, 111, 116.
10   Leiser, *"Deutschland erwache!"*, 111 et seq.
11   Leiser, *"Deutschland erwache!"*, 112, 120.
12   Kracauer, *Caligari*, 359, 510.

1   Siegfried Kracauer, *Von Caligari zu Hitler. Eine psychologische Geschichte des deutschen Films* (1948), Frankfurt a. M. 1984, S. 235.
2   Rezitiert wird aus dem „Vorspiel auf dem Theater", der ersten Szene aus Goethes *Faust*.
3   Berta Drews, Schauspielerin und Ehefrau Heinrich Georges, schildert dies in ihren Lebenserinnerungen. Berta Drews, *Heinrich George. Ein Schauspielerleben*, Hamburg 1959, S. 11 f. Vgl. auch Joachim A. Lang, *Heinrich George. Eine Spurensuche*, Leipzig 2013, S. 16.
4   Hierin ähnelt der Film der früheren Fernsehproduktion *Wenn sie mich nur spielen lassen* (Irmgard von zu Mühlen, 1997), die kurz nach der Rehabilitierung Georges durch die Russische Föderation produziert wurde. Götz George darin: „Ich finde, nach 50 Jahren sollte es keine Kritik mehr geben [...]. Wir sollten jetzt langsam in die Stunde des Feierns kommen." Vgl. auch Lang (wie Anm. 3), S. 154.
5   Erwin Leiser widmet dieser Szene eine genaue Betrachtung und folgert mit Gregory Bateson, „daß die Charakteristik der Kommunisten in diesem Film ein Selbstporträt der Nationalsozialisten ist. [...] Das ‚Schinkenklopfen', durch das die Kommunisten [...] als eine brutale und undisziplinierte Horde charakterisiert werden, wurde gerade von der Hitlerjugend in Wirklichkeit oft gespielt. Die Kommunisten werden als die Antitypen der nationalsozialistischen Ideale dargestellt, wobei die Attribute, die den Kommunisten zugeteilt werden, ihre psychologischen Wurzeln im Charakter der Nationalsozialisten haben." Erwin Leiser, *„Deutschland, erwache!" Propaganda im Film des Dritten Reiches*, erw. Neuausgabe, Hamburg 1978, S. 41. Vgl. auch Leisers Film *Deutschland erwache: Film als Propaganda des NS-Staates* (1967/68). Auch Rüdiger Suchsland ist zuletzt in seinem Film *Hitlers Hollywood. Das deutsche Kino im Zeitalter der Propaganda 1933–1945* (2016/17) auf diese Szene eingegangen.
6   Leiser (wie Anm. 5), S. 37.
7   Dies lässt an eine andere berühmte Vater-Sohn-Beziehung denken: Thomas Harlan arbeitete sich Zeit seines Lebens an der Rolle und Funktion ab, die die Filme seines Vaters für den NS bedeuteten. Hier sieht er die eigentliche Schuld und Fehlleistung des Vaters, resultierend aus Filmen wie *Jud Süß*: Wenn „Du einen Hammer gemacht hast, mit dem andere totgeschlagen [wurden], kannst Du kein Hammermacher mehr sein... Kann man noch Regisseur bleiben?" Mit dieser Resolutheit ringt er mit dem Erbe des Vaters, eindrucksvoll dokumentiert in dem langen Filmgespräch *Wandersplitter* (Christoph Hübner und Gabriele Voss, 2004–2006).
8   Leiser (wie Anm. 5), S. 79.
9   Harlan erhielt für seinen Film nicht nur alle finanziellen Freiheiten („Der Film durfte kosten, was er wollte", zit. n. Thomas Harlan, *Veit*, Hamburg 2011, S. 122), für die (später gekürzten) Schlachtenszenen wurde ihm (nach seinen eigenen Angaben) die grotesk hohe Zahl von 187.000 Soldaten zur Verfügung gestellt. Leiser (wie Anm. 5), S. 111 u. 116.
10   Leiser (wie Anm. 5), S. 111 f.
11   Leiser (wie Anm. 5), S. 112 u. 120.
12   Kracauer (wie Anm. 1), S. 235 u. 510.

Mike Terry
CLAY ALLEE BERLIN, 2012–13

Like a reality check, Mike Terry's photographs, taken between 2012 and 2013, bring us to a conclusion by documenting the brief period of intensive sales campaigns before the subsequent conversion of the office complex into condos and apartments. Piggybacking on the building's easily digestible and sellable American history, Terry's images showcase a sweetly banal situational comedy that seems as fictional as the films that were shot on the site. They underline the significance of the historical for property today, exemplifying how symbolic value was—and continues to be—converted into capital within Berlin's urban development.

Mike Terry
CLAY ALLEE BERLIN, 2012–13

Einem Realitätscheck gleich entlassen uns die Fotografien von Mike Terry, aufgenommen zwischen 2012 und 2013, die die kurze Zeitspanne des marketingstarken Verkaufs vor der anschließenden Umnutzung des bürokratischen Gebäudekomplexes in Condos und Mietwohnungen dokumentieren. Huckepack auf der leicht verdaulichen und absetzbaren US-amerikanischen Geschichte des Gebäudes zeugen die hier gezeigten Szenen von einer lieblich-banalen Situationskomik, die ähnlich fiktional erscheinen wie die Filme, die auf dem Gelände gedreht wurden. Sie unterstreichen den heutigen Stellenwert des Historischen in einer Immobilie, der exemplarisch dafür stehen kann, wie sich innerhalb der Berliner Stadtentwicklung symbolische Aufladung in Kapital hat umtauschen lassen – und es bis heute vermag.

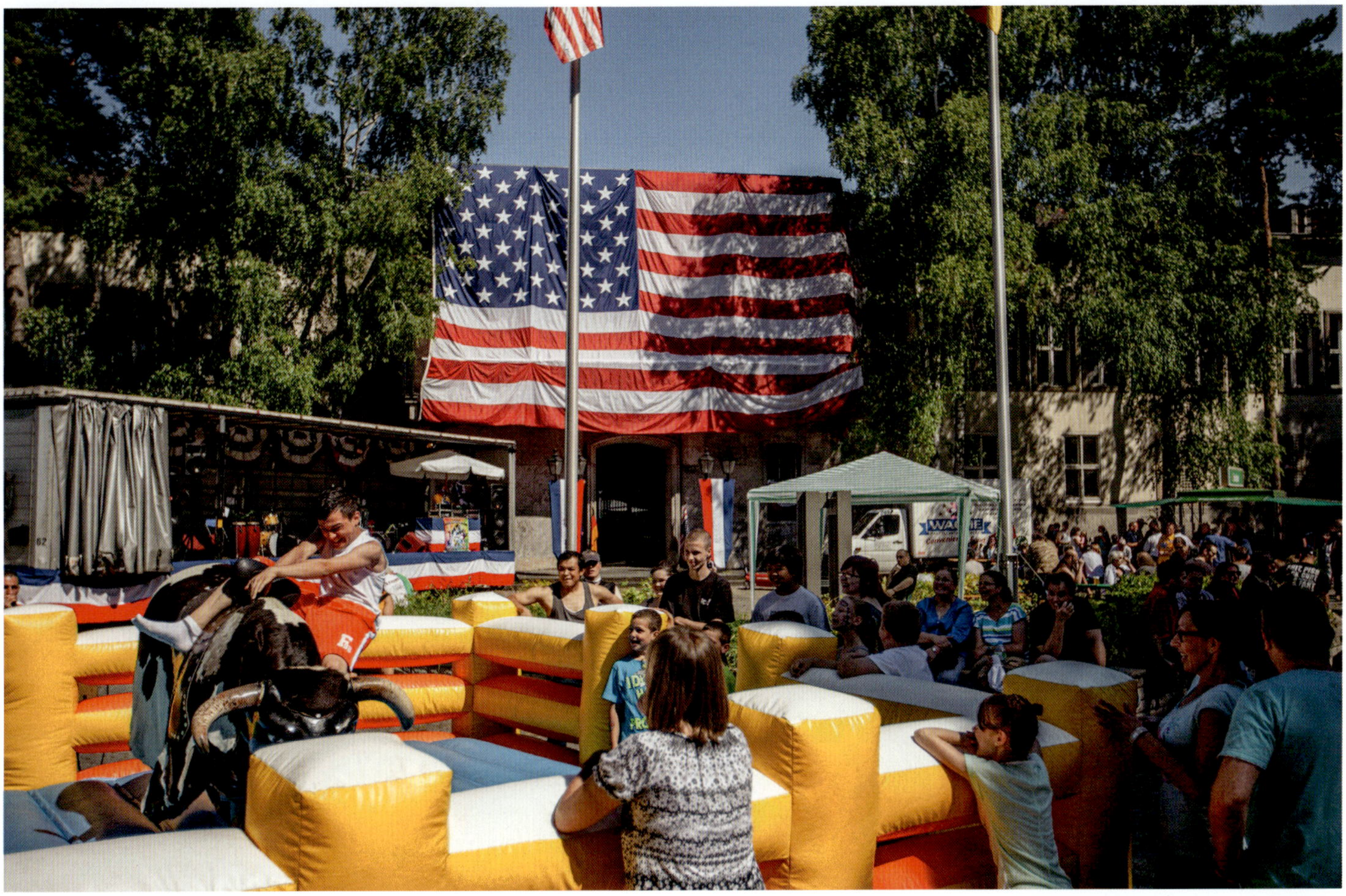

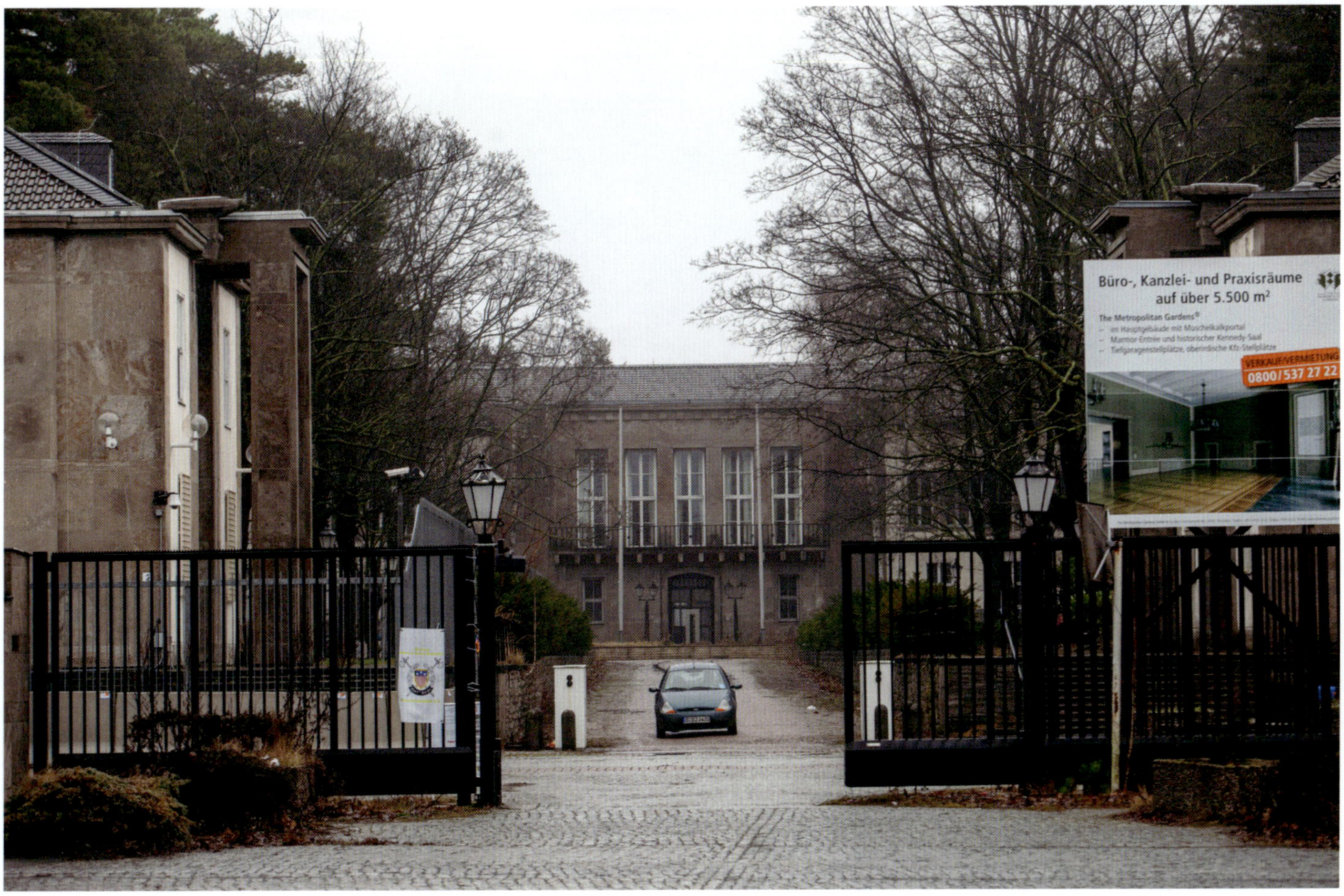

Büro-, Kanzlei- und Praxisräume
auf über 5.500 m²
The Metropolitan Gardens®
- im Hauptgebäude mit Muschelkalkportal
- Marmor-Entrée und historischer Kennedy-Saal
- Tiefgaragenstellplätze, oberirdische Kfz-Stellplätze
VERKAUF/VERMIETUNG
0800/537 27 22

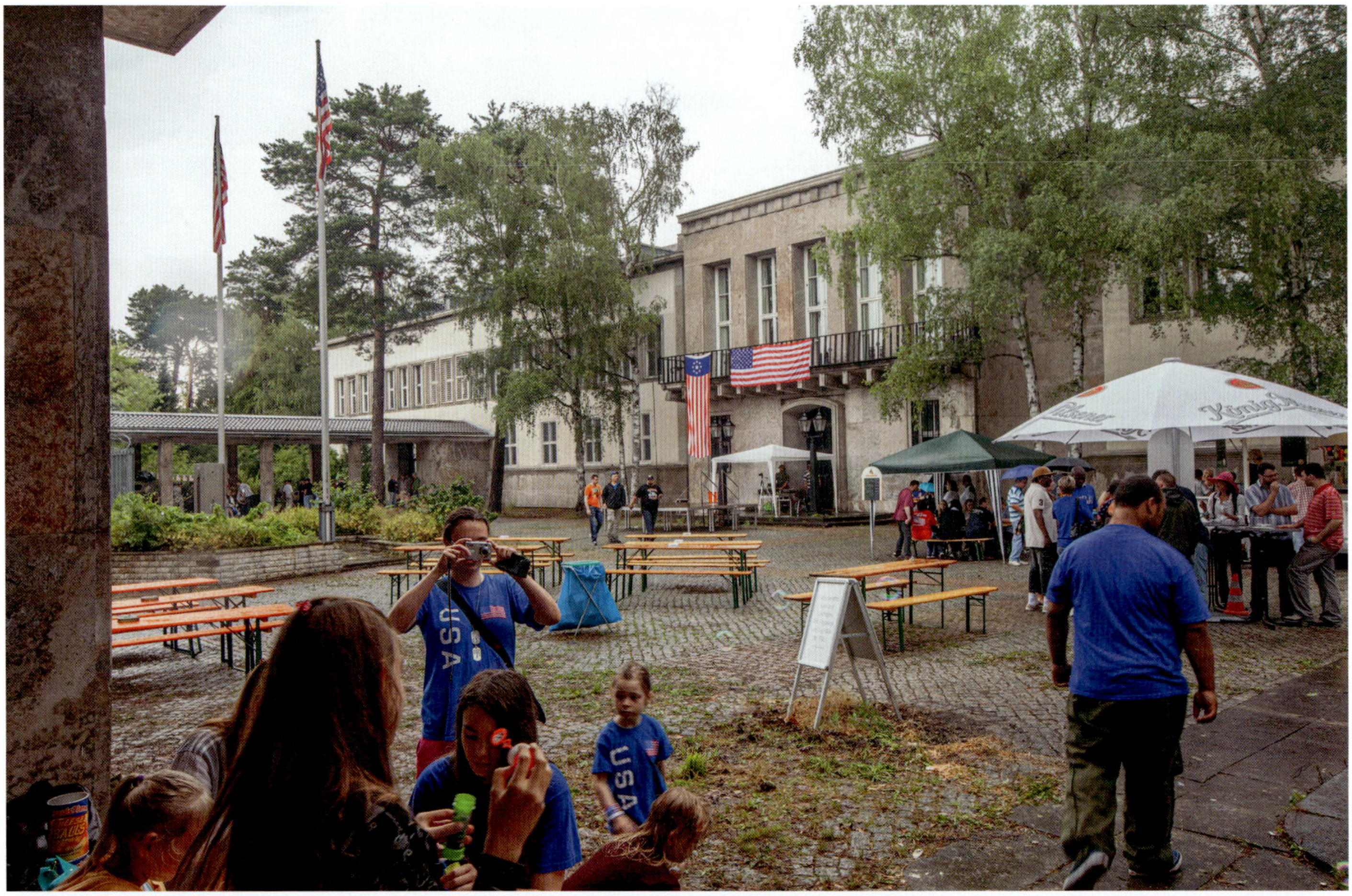

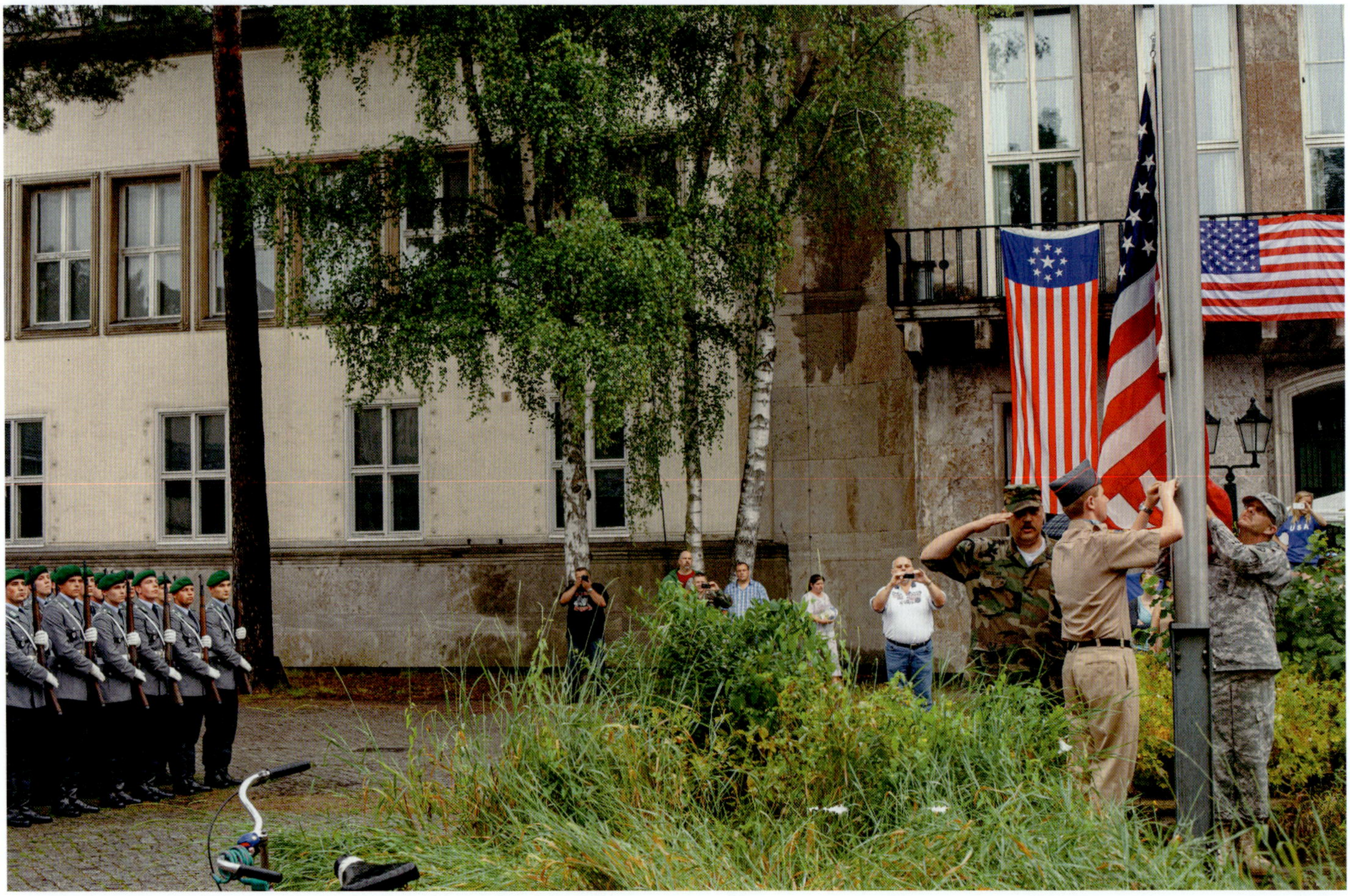